How a Mother Should Talk About Money with Her Daughter

How a Mother Should Talk About Money with Her Daughter

A Step-by-Step Guide to Budgeting, Saving, Investing, and Other Important Lessons

Aja McClanahan

ALLWORTH PRESS
NEW YORK

To my favorite money muses with love: Lodena, Sandra, Alanah, & Reagan.
You are the generations of compassion and change.

Allworth Press books may be purchased in bulk at special discounts for sales promotion, corporate gifts, fund-raising, or educational purposes. Special editions can also be created to specifications. For details, contact the Special Sales Department, Allworth Press, 307 West 36th Street, 11th Floor, New York, NY 10018 or info@skyhorsepublishing.com.

24 23 22 21 20   5 4 3 2 1

Published by Allworth Press, an imprint of Skyhorse Publishing, Inc. 307 West 36th Street, 11th Floor, New York, NY 10018. Allworth Press® is a registered trademark of Skyhorse Publishing, Inc.®, a Delaware corporation.

www.allworth.com

Cover design by Mary Ann Smith
Cover illustration by iStock

Library of Congress Cataloging-in-Publication Data is available on file.

Print ISBN: 978-1-62153-742-7
eBook ISBN: 978-1-62153-743-4

Printed in the United States of America

Table of Contents

Introduction

If you are a mom, aunt, grandmother, big cousin, schoolteacher, or have contact with women you mentor in some capacity, this book is for you. I wrote this book so that we, as women of influence, can begin to have important, compelling talks about money with the women who look up to us for advice.

I think the biggest problem we face is knowing that our personal money situation might not be perfect, so we don't feel comfortable broaching the subject with anyone, let alone any young woman who might actually take the advice we give to them. After all, what if we give them the wrong advice?

The point of this book is not so much to give advice as it is to get the conversation around money going. Just like we talk about men, relationships, beauty tips, and other "girlie" things, we can talk about money. Can you still give beauty tips out even if you are not a high-fashion model? Of course you can! Can you talk about relationships even if you've had several that failed? Yes!

The purpose of this book isn't to make you a money guru. It's designed to help you become confident when it comes to talking about money with the women you love. These can be your daughters, sisters, coworkers, friends, or any women in your life you want to pow-wow with around money.

My dream is to make money talk as common (and fun) as talking about the latest celebrity gossip, fashion, parenting, mimosa, or whatever it is you find interesting and enriching. I want to see women curl up with this book as they sip evening tea and relax from a hectic day or week.

I'd like to see women sitting on their daughter's twin bed, hand on their mini-me's shoulder while looking deeply in their eyes saying, "Daughter, let's have *the talk* about money. Here's what you need to know about me and here's what I'd like you to avoid and learn from my mistakes." Just like you'd warn her against silly boys who could break her heart, I'd want you to warn her about the financial negligence and apathy that could rob her of her future.

The point of this book is to start conversations that lead to "the village" to finally talk about and tackle serious money issues that concern women *together*. After reading this book, my hope is that you'll take what you read into your tribes and fearlessly talk about your credit score, student loans, or retirement savings at brunch—no matter how embarrassing it might feel.

Hopefully, everyone around you will be relieved that you are starting the conversation and are actually being transparent about it. Maybe they'll be happy that they can finally talk about their money stress and find some respite from what worries them. Maybe they'll learn something they never knew about.

Maybe they'll walk away feeling encouraged about their financial future. Perhaps they'll get new ideas and a fresh outlook on how to manage their money going forward. What if someone is able to craft a brand-new, well-fitting, and perfectly customized financial plan that makes them look forward to the future because of you? What if they just feel comfortable to air out their fears and concerns about money because of you?

The possibilities of the good that can come from this conversation are endless. Your bravery could be the very thing that inspires someone else to start their own money conversations in their own circles.

The stakes are just too high not to engage in the money talk we all dream of having but are just too scared to share. What better place to start than in our homes with the women on whom we have the most influence? Our daughters are part of the rising generation that will inherit a world for which we prepare them. I say, let's bring money as front and center as we would education, relationships, and career choices.

If you don't have a daughter quite yet or don't plan to, no worries. You've still got a role to play in this village-wide conversation. We all do. We've all got circles where we need to have that "come to Jesus" moment about money.

Though we've got a ways to go, I can see the seeds of change starting to bloom. I'm encouraged when I see "regular" people on Instagram talk about their money ups and downs. On one post someone might admit that they blew their carefully planned budget with weekend partying. On another, that same person might turn down the chance to buy those $600 Christian Louboutins because they're saving for a down payment on a home.

Then, of course, there's the influencer crowd whose niche is personal finance. If you follow any of them, many of them are blazing crazy trails when it comes to removing the stigma around money conversations. Even more mainstream artists and actors are touting personal financial responsibility more than ever. (Even though I feel like there's still more talk about "stunting" than saving, it seems like the tide might finally be changing.)

The way the world is more connected and coming together on topics like money gives me hope that we'll find solutions to bridge the gender wage and wealth gap sooner than later. You can be on the front lines of this trend or on the tail end trying to catch up. Hopefully, this book motivates you to be the former!

Finally, I want to tell you what money conversations did for me and my financial situation. I delivered a TEDx Talk called "Money Conversations with Our Daughters," and revealed the money conversations that changed *my* life.

My grandmother, Lodena Pouncey, was born in Mississippi and came to Chicago during the Great Migration with thousands of other

Blacks that wanted to escape the oppressive racism of the deep South. This racism was salient and far-reaching—stifling both the soul and the pocketbook.

As a youngster in Chicago, she earned money by cleaning homes for wealthy people in the suburbs. She didn't make tons of money doing it, but she managed to get married, buy a home, and build a life that would help her support both friends and family members financially for years to come.

Whenever someone needed a place to stay or new tires for their car, my granny was always able to help. In fact, when I needed a place to stay, she took me in and allowed me to live with her rent-free. She even helped me pay bills like my car note and student loans. I later found out that I wasn't the only person she helped in this way, either.

How was she able to do all of this? Until this day, I still have no idea! But I do know that she was the kind of lady that talked about money all day, every day.

She'd tell me stories of how she grew up during the Great Depression and picked cotton as a young girl. Her family was so affected by the Great Depression that she became frugal with a capital F. When living with her, I saw that she saved plastic baggies and paper towels while freezing everything from sweet potatoes to milk.

I didn't understand her frugal ways, but subconsciously I realized I was soaking them up. Not only did I absorb many of her money-saving mannerisms, I was also subject to her very direct admonishments around money and all things financial.

In my early 20s, my *modus operandi* was ignoring bills at all costs. I'd let mail pile up and ignore notices until I couldn't anymore. (I even got my license revoked once because of this bad habit.) My granny would never let me live this type of behavior down.

She'd rip open my mail and demand that I told her what was going on. She'd say, "How are you out here talking on the phone, running the streets, and having fun in your life if you've got bills to pay?"

I didn't have a good answer for her, but she'd scold me enough until I'd eventually felt guilty about ignoring bills and routinely neglecting my financial responsibilities. She'd ask me how would I run my family finances if I couldn't handle my own, as a single woman, properly. Then she'd remind me of where she came from and the obstacles that she overcame to become financially responsible. She'd tell me, "If I can pay my bills, so can you."

She'd teach me to buy in bulk, then freeze anything that could be frozen. She'd encourage me to pay ahead on bills whenever I could.

Granny was also a stickler for education. To her, it was the ultimate form of financial responsibility—getting an asset that no one could ever repossess or revoke. She always told me, "What you get up here, no one can take from you," as she peered over her bifocals while pointing to her head.

After spending more time with her, I began to understand where she was coming from. In essence, all the frugality, all the saving, all the good money habits were for the purposes of going higher and being a productive, educated member of society. It wasn't misery for the sake of misery. It was financial prudence for the sake of elevation.

Truthfully, I didn't appreciate all her money lessons at first. At the time, I was so annoyed that she wouldn't let me live and mind my business, no matter how poorly I was minding it.

However, I learned that her scolding, fussing, and setting good examples planted seeds in me that would serve me until this very day. Without even realizing it, she influenced me to study economics and is very likely the reason I'm a writer and speaker that covers personal finance and entrepreneurship.

The money conversations that she had with me changed my life. She'd tell me about her money mistakes and triumphs and even shared about the times she knew she got swindled. The conversations were open, honest, and introspective. I got to see her process and reprocess money memories so she could make sense of them and package them into advice she thought would be more useful to me. That alone was so valuable!

My Granny's understanding of financial matters wasn't sophisticated, but it was still effective. She understood that giving and generosity, according to the natural laws of mathematics, should have made her poorer. But she'd observe with awe and wonder every time she prospered because of her giving. I got to witness that, too.

Bottom line—money conversations don't have to be painful, insightful, or profound. They just need to *happen*—and happen more often. The deep revelation and mind-shattering epiphanies will come, but they still need to start somewhere. They start with thoughts that turn into words that are weaved into conversations that help us work out the best money paths for ourselves, our families, and eventually the world.

This is the gift that my grandmother gave me. For it, I am eternally grateful. This is the gift I've enclosed in every chapter of this book so you and your daughters, cousins, nieces, roommates, and powerful circles of women can do the same!

CHAPTER 1

My Money Story

As an economics major and finance writer, I get so many questions about money. People, women especially, want to know how they can manage their money better and become more financially stable.

As you may or may not know, personal finance is really very personal. It's not just numbers and equations. Though math can help inform our decisions when it comes to money, it's not the only thing that can influence how we handle money matters.

When I talk about money with people, I like to ask them about their money story. When people ask me for advice, I often share as much of my money story as I can so they can understand my perspective (which may or may not serve them very well, but I let them be the judge.)

I think sharing my money story is a way to model money transparency, and I think it will help you understand my take on money and finance. So, here's the why behind how I feel about money today.

The first time I remember learning about money and how it really affected my life was around the time my parents got divorced. Prior to that time, I don't remember my parents really talking about how expensive life was or if there was ever enough money. We'd go somewhere, and my parents would pay for whatever they needed, transacting most of their business without so much as a complaint.

I felt like I had a happy childhood in that pretty much whatever we asked for was given to us. If we wanted a toy, my parents would get it. If we had a taste for ice cream, it was not a problem to go out and grab a cone.

My grandmother loved spoiling us and taking us to McDonald's whenever we asked her to. I remember that she hated it when we wasted food but still, there was never any talk about anything costing too much or money being short.

That all changed when my parents got divorced. I believe I was around six years old when they started the proceedings. About three years went by and the divorce was final, at which point my mother purchased her own home —just a few blocks away from my dad. It was at this point that I became keenly aware of our money situation.

Though both my parents were gainfully employed as working professionals (my mom was a nurse and my dad was an engineer), they both seemed to talk much more about money and the restrictions around things we could do. Now, there just wasn't enough money to do everything we wanted to do.

Looking back, this makes sense. There were now two households to support and manage instead of one. And even years after their divorce, my parents were still in court over custody arrangements and child support. As I understand, this was pretty expensive for the both of them.

Eventually, my dad went on to start another family. He got married and had two more children. At that point, he would have to cover child support along with the cost of supporting his new family. I remember that my dad constantly complained about paying child support while my mother griped that my dad didn't give her enough money.

At this point, it seemed, that almost everything we did was dictated by the money that my parents had (or didn't have). I started to understand that it was better to eat at home than to eat out. It cost less and would help my mother stretch her paycheck longer. It was then that I began to cook so that my mother could save money on the food budget.

When my mother became a homeowner, she also became responsible for maintaining her home. She had to do repairs and things like mowing the lawn. The only problem was there wasn't always a lot of money in her budget to do that. She worked a lot and didn't have time to do it and she didn't have the money to hire anyone either. So, we picked up the slack. My brother and I began to mow the lawn.

It might sound so noble that us kids chipped in to help my mom when she needed it. But actually, we were entitled little brats that totally resented the situation. That much I remember!

We felt like we shouldn't have to do so much work and were pretty vocal about it. We didn't mince words when we talked to her about the situation. I believe this often made her feel guilty and caused her to spend more on things like clothes and special outings to make up for our "broken" home life.

That single-mom guilt guided a lot of her spending decisions and many times, she'd just be treading water financially in the name of giving us a good life. I love and respect her for her deep desires to give us so much, but I also realize that she could and should have put her foot down in some areas. Nevertheless, as a single mom, things can just be so much more difficult and complicated.

Fast forward to high school (by the time I was about 16 years old), my mom and I couldn't get along anymore and I was sent down the road to live with my dad. Of course, my dad obliged and provided me with whatever I needed while I crashed on his basement couch.

Though I lived with him and his new family, in some ways, it was like living alone. I came and went as I pleased and got into a lot of counterproductive things as a result.

Amazingly enough, I never snubbed my studies. Sure, I skipped school a lot, but I was also diligent about keeping up with my grades. My biggest motivation was getting good grades so I could finally move out and be on my own. I felt that getting good grades would get me into college, so I gave my best when it came to academics.

I had a good friend in high school, named Tiffany, who was meticulous about things like money, scholarships, internships, etc. When I didn't know what to do on this front, I just followed her lead. When she announced she was going to get a job, I did the same thing. When she got a checking account, I went and opened one, too.

By the time we were applying for college, I pretty much just copied her—applying to many of the same schools and everything. She told me all about scholarships, and we even applied to the same ones together! Tiffany was light-years ahead of her time when she suggested that we apply for internships.

Once again following Tiffany's lead, I did just that and was hired to work at a premier telecom called Lucent Technologies. At the age of 17, I was already working in corporate America and would later go on to work for Verizon as a college intern because of this experience.

Tiffany was a friend and role model to me. She saved her own money and bought a car when she was 17. When she wasn't working or interning, she was selling candy she purchased in bulk from Sam's Club in our high school. I met her when we were eight years old, and even in third grade she was trying to sell me bookmarks and friendship bracelets!

It became clear to me that money mentorship doesn't always come from parents or relatives. I was drawn to this friend because she was fun but I stuck around because she was smart and helped me get a jump-start understanding money early on in life.

I didn't totally get it though. Even though I had a number of jobs by the time I had turned 17, I pretty much spent every dollar that came into my hands. I remember getting paychecks that would be $100 or a little more (which was huge to me as a 16-year-old). Then I'd go straight to the nearest department store and spend the entire thing on one, single outfit.

One of my biggest accomplishments was earning an extra $500 in commissions as a telemarketer when I was 16 or 17. I sold the *New York Times* newspaper to people all around the country. Whenever I got people to buy a subscription, I'd get an extra commission on top of my hourly rate.

My goal was to be a top seller for that month so that I could make enough to cover everything I needed for my high school prom. To my surprise, I made the goal and I felt like I was the most accomplished person in the world.

Then, I proceeded to spend every last penny of that jackpot paycheck on my high school prom. As a result, I needed my mom to give me more money, since I went over my budget! To top it all off, I knew I was pretty short on the money I needed for college. I still thought that prom was a higher priority and had no problem making that irresponsible financial decision.

My thought process at the time was that I might be able to take out student loans for my tuition, so I didn't think that much about it. Then, my grandmother kept telling me how she'd been putting money away for me for college since I was a little baby. So I thought that there was a good chance that I'd have everything covered.

Boy was I surprised when it came time for me to go away to college. The money that my grandmother had been putting away all those years? It was a whopping $1,800!

My granny didn't know much about investing in securities like stocks or bonds, so she put the money in a low-yield money market account. Of course, she probably didn't realize the power of compound interest and probably didn't expect my college education to be almost $30,000. After all, her experience with the Great Depression likely taught her that the stock market was too risky and not worth investing in. So, I can't fault her at all. It was just the time she grew up in.

In all, I think that money *might* have just covered my books for my first semester in college. Either way, I was so thankful that she thought so much of me and saved up the money. It's something that I'm doing for my kids and I'm sure she was the one that gave me the thought in the first place.

After my first semester in college, I realized that I probably wouldn't have enough money to finish my education. I was seriously contemplating going back home and doing something else with my life. But then, I learned that I could get a private loan to cover all four years of my tuition.

The only problem was that the private lender wanted me to have a cosigner. I didn't have a strong enough credit profile or income prospects to warrant giving me a loan—even if it was for school. I asked my parents to cosign, and they declined.

My granny, though, came through and happily cosigned that loan for me. Why she had so much faith in me, I'll never know!

As soon as we both signed on the dotted line, the checks started coming. At the beginning of every semester, I'd get a refund check from my private loan money. Sometimes it would be around $1,200, and other times it could be a couple thousand.

I had no idea, but I had the option to give this money back to decrease my final loan balance. In my defense, I did use some of the money to cover living expenses that I truly had. For example, a couple of years I did stay off campus and use the money to cover my rent.

But even then, I'd have plenty of money left over. I would use that money to go shopping or take trips. Plus, I had taken advantage of the many credit card offers presented to me on the University's quad. In exchange for t-shirts, bottles of soda, and free pizza, I happily signed up for several credit cards (on which I would eventually default, but that's another story).

Some years I was working 20, 30, or even up to 40 hours a week while I was studying. During the summers I was working full time and making more than enough money to make extra payments on my student loans. Do you think I did it? No!

I was making relatively good money in college and getting all of these refund checks pretty regularly, but the thought never occurred to me to make payments toward my loan. In fact, I don't even think it occurred to me that I would ever have to pay this money back at all!

I was in for a rude awakening about six months after I graduated. By then, I had started working at my first job. I started getting bills from the bank to repay my loan. I couldn't believe they had the audacity to want me to pay back the money I borrowed.

At the time, I was making less than $25,000 a year. But I had taken on the burden of an expensive apartment in the suburbs, a new car note, and other living expenses. If I could do it all again, I'd get a cheap car with cash and stay with a relative rent-free. This would have helped me act like a responsible adult and pay the bills that I made while in college.

But I didn't. Now, I was at a loss at how I would pay this money back. The kicker was that since this was a private loan (not a federal loan) I didn't have any options for deferment or forbearance. I simply had to make payments as they came—no excuses.

Eventually, I would get overwhelmed and just start to ignore the notices. Because my grandmother was a cosigner on the loan, she began to get notices and eventually called me about them. She would ask why I wasn't paying my student loan off. I told her I just didn't have the money.

She knew I was probably just living beyond my means and really didn't care to pay the money back. She was right. But she wouldn't let me go out like that.

My granny offered to help pay my bill until I could get myself together. After a while, she even welcomed me into her home after I got tired of paying rent at my suburban apartment.

Right when I moved in with her, I quit my job and had no income—so much for that plan. But she was still patient with me and continued to help with my bills by both paying some of my bills and lecturing every five minutes about how to handle my money.

Not long after I moved in with her, I started dating my now-husband. I was ecstatic at the prospect of getting married. Looking back, I think my granny was just as excited because it meant that I could get off her payroll and onto someone else's!

She would help me put together dinners for him and got so excited when he would come visit me at her house. She was probably so ready for me to move on with my life, but she felt like she had to bring us together. After seeing him just a couple of times she started referring to him as her son-in-law. I thought that was pretty funny and sweet.

During our courtship, however, she continued to impart her financial knowledge. She'd tell me, "Make sure you all get on the same page about money. Tell him about your money situation and make sure he tells you about his."

Her sage advice did prompt me to start having those conversations with him while we were dating. I tried, the best I could, to outline the money that I owed and what kind of career path I thought I would take so that I could get it paid off. My then-boyfriend and now-husband did the same.

So far, it seemed like we both agreed that our goal was to pay off our student loan debt, become homeowners and business owners, and strive to build wealth together. Not too long after we began dating, we got married.

Our first daughter came not too long after our nuptials. This is when things got interesting. First, we both agreed that I would stay home with our daughter as long as possible. We even contemplated homeschooling her. This meant we would have to live on one income for quite some time.

The only problem?

My husband had underestimated his student loans to the tune of $20,000. Instead of having a combined $40,000 in student loan debt we soon realized that we really had $60,000 worth of student loan debt.

For hubby, one of those loans was with a private college that proceeded to garnish his wages almost as soon as we got married. Not only were we living on one income at the time, but it was being ravished by both of our student loan payments, the garnishment, and other consumer debt like my husband's car note and both of our expensive SR-22 car insurance.

My husband actually made good money, but we both happened to have made poor financial decisions. It looked like we had too much debt for our dream of being a homeschooling family. It was starting to feel like we'd never be able to meet our goal when we pitted family vision against our income.

For the sake of total transparency, I do want to add that during this time we still received a lot of family support. Both our parents and my grandmother continued to chip in and help us out when we needed it. We still had some very difficult times financially, but I do want to disclose that we also had a fair amount of help in the process.

However, we knew that this extra help was not a permanent solution to our money problems. We really wanted to get to the root of our money issues so that we could make sustained progress toward our money goals and the life we desired to live as a family.

Long story short—we both became resolute in our efforts to pay off all of our debt. We didn't do everything right, but we eventually made it our reality. The road was bumpy and filled with obstacles, but it all started when we found a plan.

As fate would have it, I had stumbled upon American's favorite debt-free guru, Dave Ramsey, while driving in the car one day. I heard him on some scratchy AM radio station talking about living a life that was free of all debt. He didn't even like it when people had a mortgage on a home. I thought he was totally and utterly insane.

I said to myself, *How could someone talk about being debt-free for 30 minutes straight? This is the most bizarre thing I've ever heard of!* I soon found out that not only did he talk about being debt-free for 30 minutes straight, his radio show was actually longer and it came on almost every single day.

I was intrigued by his antics. It wasn't before long that I picked up a copy of his book, *Total Money Makeover*. I read it in just a few hours and was totally convinced that this was the plan that could help us pay off debt so that we could homeschool our kids.

I told my husband about it and his first reaction was that it seemed a little weird that we'd be able to do it. We were already struggling and barely making it some weeks. How on earth would we be able to pay off all the debt we had accumulated?

As best I could, I explained everything I thought we needed to do in the process. He listened intently and said, "Ok, let's do it," very nonchalantly. My husband isn't very emotional, so I took that as sign that he'd be totally committed to the process—and he was!

We started by creating a budget and understanding where all of our money went. As you can imagine, even though we said we were struggling, we found that we spent a lot of money on things we really didn't need.

We ate out quite a bit, had a pretty high grocery bill, and spent a lot of money for our cable and cell phone bills. The only thing I knew to do at this point was cut back on some of these things. So we did. Then, we limited our spending on groceries and eating out. We used cash for these budget categories because that's where we tended to overspend. When the cash was gone, that was it—no going over budget or dipping into our extra cash stash. Any leftover money was used to pay down debt.

After mastering the art of frugality, we figured out that there wasn't much else to cut from our spending. The next natural step was to increase our income. The only problem was that I still wanted to stay home with our daughter. So, I started selling things on Craigslist and eBay. I could do this from home without a problem.

Then, I started tutoring and providing other support services to small business owners. I soon discovered that I was good in the area of sales and marketing. I was able to land a few consulting gigs with business owners that wanted to revamp their sales strategy and grow their sales department.

That side hustle eventually morphed into a full-scale database consultancy that I owned and worked in from home. Depending on the projects I was working on, I had anywhere from three to five people working under me. I had contractors and clients based all around the world and could work from the comfort of my own home.

This extra income, coupled with our extreme budgeting strategies, would eventually allow us to pay an extra $2,000–$3,000 per month *just* on our debt. It was exhilarating and almost unbelievable. But it was happening!

There was another fortunate, huge blessing factor that enabled us to make this happen. Our "claim to fame" so to speak, was that we moved to the inner city of Chicago to expedite our debt repayment.

Right around 2009 a relative of ours inherited a home but didn't want to move to the "hood." In fact, they knew that they wouldn't get much on the market for the house anyway, so they offered it to us.

It was paid for and would require some cleaning out and fixing up to be livable. The catch? It was located on the south side of Chicago in what is pretty much known as a gang war zone (though it's improved dramatically since we've moved in).

At first, we declined the offer. We were suburbanites and had no desire to raise our young family in the inner city. But my husband, in all his wisdom, reminded me, "We did say that we never wanted to go into debt again and that if we got a house it would have to be without debt. What if this is that opportunity?"

After some soul searching and prayer, we accepted the offer. It took us about a year to get it ready because we were using cash to renovate it. When it was all said and done, we finally moved into a mortgage-free, rent-free home.

I won't lie, we were both terrified at the prospect of living there. Friends and family warned us that we were making a bad decision.

Was financial freedom really worth our safety? It was the question we asked ourselves over and over again while we lived there.

Thankfully, our safety living there was never a problem, but it wasn't without some inconveniences.

Once, someone vandalized our air conditioning unit to get a couple dollars worth of copper from the metal recycling facility. It was during a record-breaking heat wave the entire country was experiencing. The estimates to fix it were between $3,000 and $4,000.

My husband is a letter carrier and spends his day out in the heat. Needless to say, he's a huge fan of air conditioning. At the time, we had to decide whether we'd fix the unit or continue paying off debt. Like a trooper, my husband said, "Let's pay off this debt!"

That summer was hard. We put a window unit in the room and we all piled there at night to get some relief from the heat. However, we continued to pluck away at our debt as we always had. Just a few months later, we paid it all off at the end of 2013.

In all, we paid off over $120,000 worth of debt and haven't looked back. The blessing in it all was that our daughters got to experience every moment of victory and defeat during the process. They waited, with bated breath, for the moment that we could scream, "We're debt free!"

Oh, and the "warzone" is actually transforming into an up and coming neighborhood with steadily increasing property values. Not only do we love our neighbors, but we've plugged into a great community that we are proud to call home. In fact, we just purchased a second property there with cash!

Being debt-free has allowed us to travel more as a family, too. I've taken my kids to places like California to study plant life, Cuba to study government and civics, and the Dominican Republic to learn Spanish. As I write this, we are planning a long trip to Costa Rica in a few weeks for more Spanish immersion.

I'm also able to support my daughters in their acting and entertainment career as well. My flexible schedule allows me to tote them back and forth to auditions and jobs regularly. Both my kids have been paid to act, sing, and perform voiceover work for clients like Walmart, McDonald's, Pepsi, American Girl, and more. They've learned to invest their earnings and will likely have their college education covered along with their first home or condo.

So, as you can see, it's more than possible to go from having a terrible money mentality and living paycheck to paycheck to winning with money and even setting up the next generation of money-making moguls.

Another great side effect of paying off all the debt was my blog. The process gave me the idea to start a blog so I could help others win with money. If we hadn't made the commitment to accomplish this goal, I wouldn't be writing books, speaking, and traveling so I can help people get control of their money situation.

I hope you are starting to see how your money journey and how you talk about it with others can have a profound effect on the people you love. Even if you've messed up with money, you still have something to say that can help, inspire, and encourage your daughter or any woman in your life who you want to see win with finances.

I hope that my money story has done that for you as well.

CHAPTER 2

Is Money Different for Women?

In a nutshell, yes. According to multiple studies and surveys, women are lagging behind when it comes to key "healthy money" indicators like net worth, savings balances, and even financial literacy. There are lots of theories floating around as to why this is true.

I think one contributing factor is because money is such a taboo subject among women. Women are afraid to talk about money, and it shows.

Fintech lender Earnest[1] found some telling disparities between men and women on the finance front and published a report all about it. To get the information, they anonymized and analyzed tens of thousands of loan applications for student loan refinancing. Earnest analyzed data relating to cash, investment, and debt balances for the applicants.

The study found that, on average, women have investment account balances totaling $19,541 versus $26,717 for males. The report also revealed that men had more than double the net worth of women.

---

1   New, Catherine. "How Age, Income, Degree, and Gender Affect Your Net Worth: Earnest." Earnest Blog | Money Advice for Young Professionals. EARNEST OPERATIONS LLC, June 13, 2019. https://www.earnest.com /blog/ranking-net-worth-by-age-income-degree-and-gender/.

Male loan applicants had an average net worth of $12,188 while women had an average net worth of just $5,541.

If you don't yet know about investing, you'll soon find out how important the element of time is when it comes to growing investment account balances (and eventually your net worth). The difference between what men and women have in terms of investment balances and net worth will only grow and compound if the issues contributing to these gender disparities with money are not addressed.

Earnest summed up the reasons these inequalities exist:

- Lower starting salaries (for women)
- Persistent wage gap (women tend to earn less money)
- Behavioral bias toward risk-taking (women do not invest like men)

Ellevest, an online robo-advisory company created specifically to help women invest, has similar findings. They cite an example scenario[2] of a woman and a man with bachelor's degrees who'd both earn $85,000 per year and would invest 10 percent of their salaries. According to Ellevest, at the age of 67, the women could have up to $320,000 less in investment balances than her male counterpart.

According to their research, the gender wage gap causes women to reach a peak in their salaries around the age of 40, while men reach their peak around the age of 55. This is especially problematic, as women tend to outlive men by 3 to 5 years, according Ellevest's analysis.

One surprising area where women excel financially is with giving. Not only do women out-give men when it comes to money, they also exceed men when it comes to giving their time and volunteering for causes they care about.

---

2 "Why It Matters." Ellevest. Accessed November 12, 2019. https://www.ellevest .com/personalized-portfolios.

According to a 2018 U.S. Trust Study of High Net Worth Philanthropy, 93 percent of high-net-worth women gave money to charity last year, compared to 87 percent of high-net-worth men.[3] The report also found that women were more likely to volunteer their time: 56 percent did so, compared to 41 percent of men.

Finally, the study confirmed something we always suspected when it comes to women. Comradery and teamwork are alive and well: one in four wealthy women gave to causes focused on women and girls, including women's health, violence against women, reproductive health, and girls' education and development.

Moral of the story? When women win with money, *humankind* wins. Even with meager resources, women use what they have to make the world a better place. Therefore, the cost of financial illiteracy and suppression among women is just too high.

So it's well worth the time, effort, and energy it will take to help young women of the world become more financially capable and develop proficiency in financial literacy. Of course, we hope that women excel as individuals as a result of their financial fitness, but we also know that when they do, it benefits society as a whole.

So, where do we start?

While it might make sense to begin educating women on concepts like credit scores and compound interest, I think the solution can be even simpler. I say, as women, let's just make it more acceptable and less taboo to talk about money!

It's not that we don't *like* talking about money. It's uncomfortable. It's awkward. But avoiding the issue altogether is having major negative impacts not only on women but on the world at large. Because let's face it, when women are happy and thriving, so is everyone else!

---

3 Albrecht, Leslie. "Who Donates More Time and Money to Charity—Men or Women? Here's Your Answer." MarketWatch, January 16, 2019. https://www.marketwatch.com/story/wealthy-women-give-away-their-money-and-time-more-than-rich-men-2018-10-24.

A 2015 study conducted by Fidelity measured how women view and address their finances. They also looked at obstacles that may hold them back from being more engaged, and incentives that would encourage them to take action when it comes to dealing with money and money topics.

A survey of over 1,500 women found that:

- Eight in 10 women confessed they have refrained from discussing their finances with those they are close to
- Women are 78 percent more likely to talk with their partners about health issues and 65 percent less likely to talk about investment ideas
- Women are 46 percent more likely to discuss parenting issues with their friends and 25 percent less likely to talk about spending habits

Why are we holding back when it's time to talk about something that has such a huge bearing on the outcomes of our lives and the lives of those we love?

The study found that:

- 56 percent of women said talking about money is too personal
- 35 percent of women don't want people they are close with knowing this information
- 32 percent of women said the conversations were uncomfortable
- 27 percent of women said they were not raised to talk about finances

Though money isn't the end all be all of our lives, it still plays a major role in our lives and how they will pan out. Money can dictate our quality of life and even affect our ability to realize dreams like helping others or making creative contributions to the world.

For this reason alone, it's more than worth it for women to start much-needed conversations around money. There's just too much we have to do in this world to be shy about getting our money in order!

CHAPTER 3

Money Mindset and Women

I think we can all agree that men and women are different. They think, communicate, and process life differently. The very design that differentiates the sexes is also responsible for both conflict and harmony when it comes to certain life issues. We can see this with one life issue in particular—money.

Some of these differences are learned, some of them might be instinctual, and others might even be part of our DNA. For example, there is some evidence that females' propensity for shopping might be something ingrained into our collective "ancestral memory." Though it's only a theory, it kind of makes sense.

In the early days when humans were hunters and gatherers, some scientists hypothesize that women were responsible for most of the gathering while the men were responsible for hunting animals for food. As a result, some researchers think that this pattern of behavior persists in women today when it comes to shopping and the female sex.[1] So it only makes sense that women enjoy going out looking for the best deals and gathering things like groceries, housewares, and clothing for the family.

---

1   Taylor, Philip, and Elle Martinez. "Can You Deduct 401K Savings From Your Taxes?" The TurboTax Blog, July 23, 2019. https://blog.turbotax.intuit.com /tax-deductions-and-credits-2/can-you-deduct-401k-savings-from-your-taxes -7169/.

Scientific studies even show that there are marked differences between men and women's brains.[2] These differences affect the way we communicate, recall memories, process emotions, and deal with life in general. Together, with both biological differences and the way culture shapes the ideas and behaviors of women, it's safe to say that women will have a different perspective and approach when it comes to money.

Of course, you can't generalize every woman and every man, but some of these observations you'll see tend to ring true when it comes to how men and women deal with finances.

For example, women are generally team players. For some reason, it seems like they are more likely to view their resources as shared and to be used for a greater good like raising a family or for giving to charity. As explained in *Psychology Today*, men, on the other hand, tend to be more competitive and are more comfortable operating in silos when dealing with money.[3]

I'm sure you've probably heard stories where someone's male spouse or significant other goes out and makes a major purchase or a huge decision without consulting his wife or significant other. Because of the way men view money and life, they are more likely to do this than their female counterparts.[4]

There are even differences in terms of how many women perceive their successes and failures when it comes to dealing with money. For example, when men feel successful about their career or investment accomplishments, they will credit their own cleverness. When they

---

2   Goldman, Bruce, and Gérard DuBois. "How Men's and Women's Brains Are Different." Stanford Medicine. Accessed November 12, 2019. https://stanmed .stanford.edu/2017spring/how-mens-and-womens-brains-are-different.html.

3   Mellan, Olivia, and Karina Piskaldo. "Men, Women, and Money." Psychology Today. Sussex Publishers, January 1999. https://www.psychologytoday.com /us/articles/199901/men-women-and-money.

4   Ibid.

feel they have failed, they'll blame an external factor like their financial advisor or the economy.

Conversely, when women experience success with money, they'll credit external factors such as their advisor or the economy or luck. When they fail with money, they will blame themselves.[5]

Another example is what happens when men earn more money than their spouse. They tend to believe they should control more of the family's decisions, especially when it comes to money. For men, more money equals more control, more power, and more respect. When women make more money, they almost always prefer a democratic, more diplomatic approach to making financial decisions.[6]

A group of high school students was asked about their knowledge of math and finances. The boys confidently answered that they knew a lot while the young women answered that they didn't—even though both groups had the same amount of knowledge on the subject.[7]

Culturally, differences are perpetuated between men and women because men are generally told and treated as if they have superior knowledge of financial matters. Even if they've never had formal training or parental grooming in the area of money, men are raised to believe that they know more about money and are therefore the more educated partner when it comes to money. In this case, most men will end up making money decisions for their family.

What about when it comes to matters in the workplace or in business? Men are encouraged to be go-getters, and their highly-developed sense of ambition is rewarded. Women who display the same tendencies are labeled aggressive or even called a "b*tch" for appearing too ambitious.

What's a woman to do when all she desires is financial security, teamwork, and peace in her relationships and the world around her?

---

5 Ibid.
6 Ibid.
7 Ibid.

Needless to say, we've got work to do when it comes to relaying messages to women that will help them find harmony between their ambitions, their relationship goals, and the rest of their lives.

At the end of the day, money is merely an extension of who we are. It reflects our preferences, personal principles, personality traits, and even how much love we have for ourselves. In essence, money doesn't make us, it only makes us *more* of what we already are.

With social media, there's even more financial pressure to play the part of someone living an awesome life. Because we are constantly bombarded with images of beauty and success on social media, financial matters become even more crucial. Essentially, women are pressured to look the part and spend insane amounts of money doing it.

In this sense, money becomes a reflection of how we are doing with ideas of self-love, self-worth, self-esteem, etc. While money can give you the perfect tummy tuck, it can also help you portray the perfect life to others. As my friend Toni Husbands of Debt Free Divas put it, "Money is like our adult report card. If you are doing well with money, you are assumed to be doing well with life. If you are doing badly with your money, you are assumed to be doing badly in life."

Even a woman's social status is tied to the financial status of the man she marries. Once people find out she's married, they'll soon inquire about her husband's occupation so they can assign her a "social value." At the very same time, women are encouraged to increase their own financial literacy and financial independence so they don't actually need a mate for financial stability.

The messages can be confusing. If you're too dependent on your husband financially, you're labeled a "kept woman" or a "lady of leisure." If you're too independent, you might threaten any prospects for marriage or a serious relationship with a man because you can do it all yourself.

The pressure to get "As" on your adult report card is ever present and ever elusive at the same time. What constitutes financial success for one woman might look totally different for another. So how can we communicate money principles to our daughters without relaying the unrealistic, confusing expectations that can be attached to them?

Setting the Narrative for Our Daughters Early On

Now that we are aware of some of the toxic norms that have been established when it comes to women and money, it's time to change them. It sounds like a massive job, and it is.

The good news is that we can change the money narratives for our daughters as we change it for ourselves. In order to destroy the mental strongholds that have convinced us of our financial incompetence, we'll have to be intentional. Reprogramming ourselves will be a long process and an intense journey, but it has to happen.

Though the truth might be that we don't know as much as we should about money and we haven't made the best decisions with our finances, that doesn't mean we can't change. Changing doesn't mean that you have to get a degree in finance or become some Wall Street money mogul.

One of the best ways we can change our personal money narrative is simply by changing the way we talk about money. Think about what happens when you get around your best girlfriends or any women that are close to you. What happens when you all begin to talk about money?

Many times, the conversation turns into the "pain" Olympics. We gripe and complain about how much money we don't have, how expensive everything is, and how we are just scraping by. We might even pass the blame onto other people in our lives—our mothers, fathers, children, a toxic mate, and the list goes on. We'll even blame the sitting president for our personal economic woes!

Not only do we gripe and complain, but we may be inclined to make the whole thing comical. We'll make jokes like, "I'm so broke I can't even pay attention." We'll share memes on social media so that we can commiserate with our online friends about the state of our brokenness.

Now, I'll be the first to admit that I've done all of these things. Sharing a meme with social media can be a way to laugh about a situation in order to keep you from crying about it. And when others chime in, it makes the experience not so isolating and more universal so that we don't feel too bad about ourselves.

At some point, however, we have to claim victory over our personal finances with our own mouth. If we're not mindful about our conversations, we can talk ourselves right out of the possibility of improving the way we manage our money.

Changing our personal money narratives so that we can do the same for our daughters starts with the conversation that we have with ourselves and with those around us. Instead of telling yourself, "I've always been bad with money. That's not my strong suit," revise your language and say instead, "I've been bad with money in the past, but I am going to do what I can to make sure I learn more about money and finances and do better." Change the, "If it's not one thing it's another," statement for something like, "I'm going to start putting away money so that I'm always prepared for emergencies."

Remember, our daughters are listening to our self-talk. As we think and reason aloud, we are showing them how to solve problems as it relates to money. If they are always listening, what do we want them to hear?

Is this some magical formula to make you a financial genius? No, of course not! In fact, nothing may seem to change for a very long time with your finances.

While you're waiting for your savings to pile up, your credit score to increase, or your net worth to skyrocket, change your language and your internal self-talk. With this change in language, you can actually change your life. You can use your words to reprogram your subconscious mind so that it leads you in a direction you actually want to go in life and, more specifically, for the purposes of this book, the direction you want to go with money.

When you become more intentional about your speech, it will naturally flow into your other conversations and other parts of your life, too. When you meet with your friends, instead of everyone competing to prove how terrible your money situations are, you'll start to redirect the conversation toward solutions and positive statements about money.

The same will happen when you're in your "comfortable place"— like at home or with those who are closest to you. Your positive self-talk will flow into conversations with your daughters. Instead of telling them, "I don't have money for _____," you'll say something to the effect of, "That's not in the budget for this month, but let's brainstorm and figure out a way to find that money or make money or save money so we can pay for _____."

This type of statement does two things. First, it puts boundaries in place so that your daughter is aware that you are changing the habit of impulse spending. You may have modeled this type of behavior for her before (i.e. in the form of Starbucks or Chick-fil-A a on a whim), but now, you're developing a habit where you plan out your spending so that you have enough to reach your monthly goals and beyond.

Second, positive statements about money let your daughters know that even though money is a finite resource, there's always a way to get more by being creative and resourceful. This way, your daughters won't feel as though their dreams and desires are impossible.

You are giving them permission to have wants and desires while setting guidelines on the best ways to go about attaining them. Yes, you can have a pony if you like, but it can't take away from your school tuition money. If you want a pony, think of the different ways that you can make extra money to buy the pony, have a place to store it, and make sure that it is cared for.

I remember when my kids were very little they would constantly ask for things when we'd go to the store. I'd tell them nonchalantly, "I don't have money for that." But then I realized I didn't like how limiting that statement sounded. (Now I can hear all you old-school parents saying what's the big deal? Kids don't need everything they want!)

While this is true, I still felt very uncomfortable letting the words, "I don't have money," out of my mouth. Again, I'm trying to change my money narrative and do the same for my daughters.

So then I figured out that saying, "It's not in my budget but let's think about another way to get it" was much more effective and put the onus upon them to take initiative and figure out how to get what they want in life.

One time, my oldest daughter asked me if we could take a plane to go see her best friend in Oklahoma. At the time, we were knee-deep in aggressively paying down debt. I was side hustling from home and homeschooling the girls. As a result, we were living on about one income (I guess I added about "half" of another income with my earnings). I was really tempted to laugh hysterically and say, "Do you know how much money that's going to cost? I don't have it!"

Instead, I chose to consciously change our money narrative by saying, "Plane tickets to Oklahoma weren't in my budget this month, but why don't we figure out a way that you can earn the money so you can go?" At the time, my daughter was six, so either I was going to get a very ridiculous response from her or she was just young enough to believe anything.

Fortunately, she was young enough to believe anything and simply responded, "Okay Mommy." She wasn't mad and didn't feel like I deflected conversation just to ignore her request. She accepted the challenge and we came up with the idea to give some money in church and pray over the money and call it a "seed" for plane tickets to Oklahoma.

Just a few weeks later she got a call from her agent. She was requested to go on an audition for a national TV commercial for a major retailer. It was so last-minute that we almost missed it. She was one of the last girls to go through the audition door. She was in there for about three minutes.

Sure enough, the very next day, she got a call from her agent telling her that she had booked the national TV spot!

For those of you who are unfamiliar with how national TV spots work, actors get paid a session fee for showing up and filming. If the TV commercial airs, they are also paid residuals for every time the commercial airs. This particular TV commercial was for the holiday season so it didn't air very long, but my daughter made thousands of dollars for her day's worth of work!

It was just enough to cover some of her acting expenses like union fees and headshots along with her plane ticket to Oklahoma! Until this day, I am still in awe of how everything panned out. When I told my daughter that we would figure out a way to get the money, I knew it would take some significant brainstorming to come up with a plan.

Of course, as a parent, sometimes you say things so that your kids can leave you alone. But then there was a part of me that was sincere when I told her, "Let's figure this out." Honestly, I thought that she would bake some cookies or make some friendship bracelets and save up for two years to go to Oklahoma.

What ended up happening was well beyond what I thought would take place. Now, that experience is forever etched in her mind. She'll always remember the time that Mommy told her, "We may not have the money now, but let's figure out a way to get it."

Even if you can't provide your daughter with an agent or help them book TV commercials, the point is that where there's a will there's a way. Even if it looks like resources are slim to reach a goal, know that determination and ambition can pick up the slack much more that the I-could-never-do-this sentiment could.

Even to this day, we go through the same thing every time my daughters tell me they want something. I'll be the first to admit that this is a lesson you may have to teach over and over again. God knows that I've done it with my kids.

But once I reiterate, "Hey, let's try and get the money," my kids remember that one awesome story and their creative juices kick in so they can get whatever thing or experience they are pining for at the time.

Between both of my girls, they've both had lots of great experiences with trips all around the country, trips outside of the country, gadgets, and even regular everyday needs like buying toiletries or hair products. I buy very little for them. When it comes to all that extra stuff like iPhones or similar electronics, I'm always encouraging them to be creative, find a way, and get it themselves.

My hope is that this process changes their money narrative. I know it has also changed mine. This is just an example of how you can change the way you think about money.

When to Start the Money Conversation with Your Daughters

After reading this, you might be thinking that you're so excited to talk about money along with dreams and visions of the future with your daughter. But you're kind of concerned because your daughter is all of two years old right now.

You might wonder, "When is a good time to talk to my daughter about money?" The truth is that you'll want to start as soon as possible and you'll probably never stop talking about it with her for the rest of your life.

I heard someone once say that you can begin teaching children about financial concepts as soon as they're old enough to say that they want something. For example, if you're at the grocery store and your child reaches out for something, they've displayed a desire or a want.

When this happens, you can start to explain financial ideas and concepts to them. Let's say they want a candy bar. Instead of snatching it out of their hands and saying, "No no no you can't have that," you can tell them, "That costs money. We will need to find enough money to buy that item."

Having this conversation with a two-year-old might make you cringe at the thought of their reaction. I'm not going to guarantee they won't throw a full-on temper tantrum in the store. But I will tell you that being brave enough to broach the subject with a two-year-old that might have a meltdown in the store will be worth it in the long run.

What you're doing is sowing a tiny little seed about money concepts. We all know that with children, you might need to say things to them a thousand times or show them one million times before they finally get it.

Once the meltdown is over and you didn't concede to getting the candy bar, you can take another less hostile time to give your daughter a piggy bank where she can store money she earns by doing chores around the house. This gesture lets her know that Mom is going to help her save enough money for her candy bar or whatever else she might want.

From here, you should keep going. I keep introducing money concepts that are age-appropriate—and believe me, there are so many that you'll never run out of material. There are plenty of financial concepts to introduce in your chats and conversations with your daughters:

- Saving
- Investing
- Giving
- Earning money
- Having a job
- Starting and running a business

- Tax strategies
- Insurance
- Estate planning
- Investing in training, education, etc.

Here are some ideas to get you started:

- Save, spend, give money jars
- Junior savings account
- Investment account
- Stockpile gift cards
- Weekend lemonade stand

There are so many ideas and financial concepts to explore that you'll likely spend the entire 18 years they're slated to be with you focusing on them. And remember, just because you go over a particular topic once doesn't mean you won't have to go over it time and time again.

Kids are funny like that. You try to tell them something and they act like they don't absorb it. Then, ten years later . . . bam! They become a genius on something about which they fought you vehemently just a few years before.

When you're dealing with young women, you'll have the extra bonus of the mouthy attitude and a young lady who thinks she knows it all. You'll be tempted to throw up your hands and give up several times throughout the process. But don't give up on her. Just think about how boneheaded you were as a young woman and teenager—then try to be patient with the one right in front of you.

Leaning into your relationship will be key. Your daughter will trust you, and your insight in money matters if you can prove your trustworthiness in other areas. Build your relationship with her first, and then insert money matters in a fun, interactive, and exciting way. Trust me, it will be well worth the "trouble" to persevere with these conversations and lessons.

The long and short of it is that you need to start having conversations around money and money concepts early on and as much as possible. Then you'll continue pretty much until forever. Even if you're learning as your daughter is learning, that's okay too.

In all of this you'll be teaching "hard" skills when it comes to money, but don't forget to teach the "soft" skills and concepts too. Remember, money is not the end goal. The freedom that money brings is.

When you talk money concepts with your daughter, do so by emphasizing that money will help you reach the other goals that you have. You can encourage your daughters to pursue things they're passionate about while being financially stable in the process. No more starving artists here!

You can talk to your daughters about standing up for themselves and demanding their value—whether they are an employee or have their own business. Their skills and talents are worth real money, and they should get paid top dollar because of what they bring to the world.

Don't forget to teach your daughters that in all this money talk, the whole goal is to create their own story. They should be able to live how they desire using the resources they are able to gather on the way through it.

Hopefully, your money talks are not dry and boring. Honestly, some of them just will be. My hope for you is that many of them will be rah-rah sessions that get your daughters excited and hyped for every stage of their life—from their first job as a teenager to being a retired grandmother that spoils her grandchildren.

All of this is possible when they envision it, plan for it, and take the actions to make sure their plans come to pass. If you frame the conversations from this perspective, it can actually be fun to talk about saving, investing, and even tax-loss harvesting. I promise!

CHAPTER 4

I'm Bad with Money; I'll Be a Bad "Money Role Model"

Getting to the heart of the money matter requires that we face our own issues and insecurities when it comes to finances. While writing this book, I requested that women submit their own money stories to me so we could get the conversation going online. I told them that the stories could be ones where the outcome was victorious or otherwise.

Someone responded, "But my story is so pitiful. Do you even want that?" I answered with a resounding yes. Many times, we are bombarded with stories of success when it comes to money, especially in the age of social media. What we don't hear about as often is when people fail with money.

Those are the stories that we need to hear, to break down barriers and remove the isolation that can come with feeling like you failed with money. So when it comes to starting conversations with your daughters around money, don't be afraid to start with the ways that you failed with money.

Some of the stories might be altogether embarrassing. But guess what! Your daughter, niece, or money "mentee" will appreciate your transparency. It may even help them open up about some difficult money issues they are facing but may have felt too embarrassed to talk about.

Many times, we don't open up about money issues because we feel like we are the only ones making huge mistakes with money. It just becomes too painful to reveal what we are going through, especially if the situation was due to a poor decision on our part. Hiding in isolation can cause us to go even deeper into depression and, consequently, back into a cycle of poor money-making decisions.

The good news is that we can stop the cycle just by having open, honest conversations that can be cathartic for ourselves and those we are sharing with.

When you start the conversation with money failures, don't stop there. Take it a step further and talk about any successes that you've had with money—even if they were very small. It's okay to talk about the time that you made some extra money on the side or were able to negotiate a bill down—even if you just saved $5, it's a win!

Talking about small wins is so important to having healthy money conversations. There's a scripture in the Bible that says, "Do not despise these small beginnings . . ." (Zechariah 4:10, NLT).

In other words, great victories must start with small wins.

Psychologically, small wins do two things. First, they challenge us to reorient our perspective. You might feel down about your experience with poor money management. Reflecting on small wins help you to change your perspective on how you're doing with money. Maybe you are still deep in debt with a terrible credit score, but if you managed to pay off just $100 of it last month, you're still technically getting better at managing your money.

Then, small wins encourage us to keep going. Maybe you only put 2 percent of your salary into your retirement account last year, but this year you are poised to put 3 or 4 percent in your retirement account. Attaining and recognizing small wins helps you gain the confidence to continue improving how you manage your money.

Even if you feel like you don't have even small wins, you probably do. You'll just have to search a little and change your mind to see the positive in your situation. When you start sharing it with others, you'll start believing that you are indeed getting better with money and you'll probably encourage yourself and someone else in the process.

If you don't feel like you are winning with money, that's okay too. It might take time to see the silver lining in your financial clouds. But even so, you can share your plans to improve your financial situation. Today you can't see anything positive or even a small win, but you can share how you are being proactive to change your financial future anyway.

These are just a few of the ways that we can start having money conversations with our daughters even when we are not experts or haven't made much progress with our own finances. Through candid, introspective conversations about our money situations, our daughters will witness our own process of reflection and analysis when it comes to money. This is something that not even money can buy!

And this is one of the major ways that we can change the narrative when it comes to talking about money. It doesn't have to be all roses and lollipops. It can be the good, the bad, and the ugly, as long as we commit to giving it a voice with an audience who stands to benefit from it.

How Much Should I Share about My Money Situation?

I have some ideas that can help you figure out what to share about your personal money journey and when. But before I do so, let me tell you a story.

My mother was a nurse and worked for a hospital as a main job and then at a few different agencies on the side. So, her checks would sometimes come in when the bank was closed. When I was around 6 or 7 years old, my mother took me with her to cash her check at the currency exchange.

I got curious and asked her, "How much money will you get when you cash this check?" I remember the look of hesitation on her face. As a mother, she probably wanted to start having the money talk with me early but wasn't sure if she should share with me how much money she'd be getting.

After a brief pause, she told me okay I'm going to tell you, but this is my business and should be kept between us. I beamed with pride as my mother finally decided to entrust me with this information. She told me the amount and I can't remember exactly how much it was— maybe it was for $400, $500, or $600.

I was shocked. That was a huge amount of money in my eyes, and I couldn't believe that someone I knew personally would soon be in possession of that amount of money. When she told me, I could hardly wait to share the news. As fate would have it, there was a random guy walking into the currency exchange just as we were. I couldn't help myself, but I remember shouting to him, "Hey, do you know my mom is about to get $500?!"

Thankfully, my mother spared my life that day. I got a brief scolding and we went on our way. But I knew she was mad. I remember the exasperated look on her face.

Initially, she knew it wasn't a good idea to tell me that information, but she was probably desperate to talk to me about money. So she ended up sharing something with me that might have been a little too premature.

Not too long after this event, my mom and dad got divorced. And as I mentioned, this is when I became keenly aware of the money issues both my parents faced. But it was all through observation. Sure, my parents complained and accused each other of being unfair with money during and after the divorce. But no one ever sat me down and said, "This is our messed-up money situation; this is how you can avoid it."

Truthfully, I ended up learning about how to deal with money only so that it causes the least amount of pain. I know that was a direct result of my parents' not knowing how to instruct me around money. They never got that instruction, so we were all just flailing around in the dark anyway.

To get back to my point about what you should say where and when. I think it will depend on your particular situation, your daughter's age, and what you need them to know about your money situation.

A personal finance friend of mine, Tela Holcomb, of the Trade Your 9 to 5 program, told me that her mother actually gave her the checkbook and routinely let her pay all the bills for the household. As a teen, she knew exactly how much money came into her house and where it went in order to keep the household running.

At the time, she thought it was drudgery and one of the worst chores imaginable. But as a successful six-figure swing trader, she knows that it was this training that helped her become good with her finances and even retire from full-time work before the age of 30.

In my case, by the time I was fifteen years old, my mother had given me her debit card and the keys to her car (yes, I drove illegally), where I'd run errands and go grocery shopping for her. I didn't pay all of the bills like Tela, but I feel as though it gave me deeper insight into what it took to support a household, money-wise. I think that experience also laid the foundation for our massive debt payoff and enabled me to start a business and create a real estate investing venture with my husband.

All this to say that you can eventually get to a point where your daughters know a lot more about you and your money situation than you'd ever imagine that you share with them. But you still might be wondering, "Where exactly do I start?" You could be sitting at home with your three-year-old daughter thinking, "What should I share and how much detail should I go into with her?"

Honestly, this is a question that you'll have to answer yourself. What you should share and how much detail you should go into will depend on your circumstances. If your money situation involves some difficult topics and close relatives, you'll focus less on details, names, etc. and more on teachable moments and somewhat abstract money concepts.

Should you share with your two-year-old that your family is declaring bankruptcy because Daddy has a gambling problem? That's probably not a good idea.

Not only would your two-year-old be confused about what bankruptcy means, but she'd have no reference point or understanding to process that kind of information. And if you're going to tell the story in a way that causes your two-year-old to be afraid of Daddy or not like him anymore, then you definitely don't want to go down that path.

I remember feeling confused about when and how to talk to my girls about sex. My oldest daughter was three years old when I got pregnant with my second child. She started to ask me where babies came from, and boy did I get nervous.

On one hand, I knew that I shouldn't avoid the conversation because even as a three-year-old, it was possible that she would start to hear things about sex anyway. But on the other hand, I didn't want to pique her interest in a topic that I felt was well beyond her years.

A dear friend and mentor helped me out by saying, "Tell your child just enough to satisfy their curiosity." It was such a relief to have a solid strategy. It actually worked for years and years.

When my three-year-old asked me where babies came from, I could confidently tell her, "Babies come from the birth canal." At three years old, she was more than satisfied with that explanation and asked hardly any follow-up questions.

About a year later, you know what her next question was. "Mommy, how does a baby get into a mommy's birth canal?" It was at that point that I could tell her, "A daddy puts the baby into a mommy's birth canal." Again, she was satisfied with that answer.

I'm sure you can imagine that the questions got more and more specific. And yes, I was nervous about finally having to explain how the birds and bees work. However, this strategy bought me time until we were *both* ready to talk about how everything worked with sex and reproduction. By the time we had this conversation, it was a little awkward, but it wasn't as painful as I envisioned because we were leading up to it anyway.

You can also take the same approach when talking to your daughters about money. Women tend to have some of the stickiest situations when it comes to money matters. If you are a woman and a mother that has been married, divorced, had kids later in life, or some other unique situation due to womanhood and motherhood, there's probably a lot of explaining you have to do when it comes to your money situation.

For example if you are divorced, money naturally becomes part of the conversation. Maybe your divorce was especially difficult or painful and even centered around hard money issues like bankruptcy, addiction, etc. I can assure you that this will be a very difficult conversation to have with your daughters.

But if you take the approach I mentioned above, you can start to be real with your daughters early on without tainting their innocence or even other relationships that may have been affected in your difficult money situation.

Maybe you have a strained relationship with your own mother because she opened credit cards in your name or committed other types of fraud in your name (this is not as uncommon as you might think). You'll be tasked with trying to have this conversation in a way that informs your daughters about your current financial situation, yet shelters their love for their grandma.

You'll also want them to form their own opinions about their grandmother. So you'll want to use language that is not incriminating or infused with negative emotion toward your mother. As much as possible, stay neutral by stating the facts and letting them ask questions according to their level of understanding.

If your current financial situation is due to an ex-spouse and involves mismanagement or betrayal, you'll still want to tread lightly. If your ex-spouse is also a father to your daughters, that relationship, as long as it's safe for them, should be protected. It's best to leave the emotion out of this conversation, though it will be hard. The main goal here is to have a healthy, teachable money conversation—not an ex-husband-bashing conversation.

In each of these situations, it's still a good idea to talk about ways that your daughters might avoid these situations in the future. This is a great time to discuss some of the warning signs that you saw (and maybe ignored) early on in these relationships or how you reacted which might have aggravated the situation.

You can take responsibility for your part of the problems you've experienced, too. When you do this, your daughters are more likely to see that they have more control over their financial destiny than they may have previously thought. Yes, some terrible things might have happened with you and your money situation that had to do with other people. But you had your part in it too. And you still have your part to play as you're trying to fix the situation even until this day.

This is an aside, but I think it's worth mentioning. When dealing with other people that have hurt you with financial matters, I think it's also helpful to address the idea of forgiveness. Because at the end of the day, staying bitter and operating out of such bitterness will only hurt you and not them.

I think it would be a wonderful thing to explain to your daughters that you forgive those that have hurt you in a way that has affected or negatively impacted your finances. You can also explain that when you forgive someone, that doesn't mean you have to trust them again in the same way.

For example, if you've ever fallen victim to financial scams at the fault of someone in your family, you can totally forgive them, but you don't have to trust them with certain areas of your life ever again. You can still love them, still forgive them, and still desire the best for them without giving them access to parts of your life that can affect your finances.

Make sense?

While you're talking to your daughters about the difficulties you had with money, don't forget to talk about what's gone right, too. As I mentioned in the previous chapter, many women tend to underestimate how smart they really are with money. If they experience success with money, they might chalk it up to luck or being in the right place at the right time.

Try to find the bright side and the silver lining in every story you have to tell about your finances. For example, when I tell my girls about all the student loan debt that I took out for college, I also mention that my college experience was a good one and helped shaped me into the person I am today. Majoring in economics, studying abroad, and meeting people that I still stay in touch with made my student loan debt more of an investment.

I also talk about how I was hardworking in high school. Sure, I didn't know much about saving money, but at the very least, I knew how to earn it. I started in food service then moved up to office jobs and eventually made it to corporate America at the age of 17.

I remember going from job to job until I landed a great internship that I was really proud of. Even when I was in college, I worked at a number of telemarketing agencies and usually out-earned my coworkers and got promoted very quickly.

Though I was proud that I made all that money in my younger years, I was still pretty bummed that it never occurred to me to pay for college out of pocket—which I totally could have done. But I still recognized my work ethic and made sure that I relayed this part of the story to my girls.

I think it's encouraging for them to know that even as young women, they have agency over their work ethic. No matter their age, they can start a career and have the power to make their own money and do with it what they choose.

Yes, I've had many money fails, but I've also had the money triumphs, too. And so have you. So make sure that you make these successes a part of your money conversations with your daughters.

Choosing to Chat

You might think that money is one of the last things that you want to talk about with your daughters. Maybe you'd rather go to the dentist or spend a day at the DMV. The truth is that we're always talking about money in some form or another.

Mostly, we talk about money on payday—how there's never enough of it—or we complain about some aspect of our lives being too expensive. Though those are the money conversations that we are having with ourselves, note that our daughters are eavesdropping. Thus, those conversations can sometimes do more harm than good, as they're not usually intentional and therefore our choice of words can be off-putting.

My challenge to you is to begin having intentional, teachable conversations about money with your daughters. Try to put away the complaining and the negativity when you bring up money. That negative energy will be relayed to your daughters! You don't want them to have anxiety about money. You'd rather them be levelheaded and take a problem-solving approach when money issues come up. That's not a natural reaction to financial problems. But we can make it more commonplace if we model that behavior in front of our daughters.

You don't have to schedule some big event or plan anything around your money chats. In fact, you can find instructional moments all around you. You can take everyday conversations that you're already having with your daughters and turn those into teachable money moments.

Just take a look at the news or pop culture headlines. There's almost always something noteworthy that can be tied back to money. For example, my daughter might be perusing the Internet or looking at YouTube for the latest celebrity scoop. More than likely, she'll find commentaries about some superstar or influencer that did XYZ. You better believe that there is a money snippet that can be drawn from that.

Once, my daughter and I started talking about how celebrities are able to dress nicely and always have on makeup based on a video she was watching. This was a great conversation for us to have because she's expressed desires to me about wanting to look "camera-ready."

It was then that we started talking about how these celebrities are paid to stay camera-ready. That's their business, so they probably also have a team of people they pay to help them run the whole operation. When they purchase clothing or put on makeup, it's more of an investment, whereas when the average Joe does it, it's purely for fun. The average Joe needs to make sure he or she has enough cash to cover his or her expenses with enough left over for luxuries like designer clothing. Otherwise, the average Joe could end up going broke trying to look like a rich person.

At this point, my daughters and I agreed that it would be a better use of our time and money to look for income-producing assets to help support the lifestyle both my daughters think they are destined to live. (You know, the celebrity influencer lifestyle!)

Of course, you don't want to turn *every* conversation into a money talk, but it is important to keep it top of mind because it will end up dictating so many things in your daughter's life. Your daughter could complain if it feels like you divert every discussion to money, so do it with discretion and in a way that you both feel comfortable with.

My Real Financial Situation

This is for those of you who have older daughters, maybe even ones who are in college or have already moved out of the house. This can be an especially sensitive subject, but I think it's worth a mention especially because it's something that I'm going through myself as a daughter.

As of this writing, I've been tasked with caring for my mom and handling her finances as well. Due to illness and other circumstances, she had to retire from her job earlier than she anticipated. About a year after retirement, she was diagnosed with breast cancer.

I have siblings, but for various reasons, I am the one who has ended up caring for her and managing her affairs. It has been hard because I didn't know much about her retirement savings and other bills. It was something we had almost never talked about.

Admittedly, I was scared to take over everything for fear of making a mistake and getting overwhelmed. I'm still managing her affairs today and I can think of a zillion things I want to share with my kids to make this easier for them should they end up in the same situation with me or their dad.

My kids are still young (10 and 14 as of this writing), but I know I still need to talk to them about my own finances. It's going to be hard, though. Money is almost always the last thing you want to talk about, especially with your kids.

As our parents age, it is inevitable that their offspring will need to know more about their financial situations when it comes to retirement and living out their golden years. Why does it seem as though people never talk about these things? For one, it has been thought of as personal business. And for another, many people don't like to talk about issues that make them face their own mortality.

Do yourself and your children a favor—start this conversation as early as you can. (If your children are younger, talk with someone you'd appoint as their guardian should something happen to you.) It might feel uncomfortable to talk about your money situation as it relates to retirement—especially if you feel ill-prepared for it. Maybe you haven't saved a lot or have failed to map out how your retirement will look. That's okay.

Even in your insufficiency, you will be doing a wonderfully considerate thing by making your daughters privy to this information. This way, they'll know how to support you should you need help and you will know what moves you need to make to better prepare for events like retirement, incapacitation, and even death.

It probably won't be a fun conversation, but at minimum it should cover things like:

- How you are saving for retirement (accounts, assets, etc.)
- Types of insurance you have and perhaps still need to put in place
- How you envision your retirement years looking
- The resources and monthly income you'll need to make that retirement lifestyle a reality
- Where you are lacking in your retirement plans and how you'll fix it

In this conversation and other money conversations, don't forget to:

- Be honest about your money mess and your plans to fix it
- Be honest about your money triumphs
- Be intentional about having money conversations
- Disclose (as age appropriate) your own money situation (i.e. salary, savings, retirement, etc.)
- Use speech that empowers your money situation (your daughters will take notice)
- Take your daughters along on your money redemption story

CHAPTER 5

Let's Talk Current Money Issues

If your daughters are anything like mine, it seems like they want things all the time. If you're living in the United States, you probably have a very decent quality of life. Your family probably has more disposable income and access to credit than you know what to do with.

Think about it—when was the last time you actually had to tell your child no?

We live in an especially prosperous time in history. We live in a well-to-do country and most of us probably live in well-to-do neighborhoods. Though we might not consider ourselves to be among the upper echelons of society, we probably still live better off than our parents or grandparents did.

It's the perfect recipe for an entitled generation. The entitlement can take on many forms including people feeling as though they are owed something or kids being outraged when they don't get what they want.

On the flip side, it feels good to be a provider for your kids. Giving them things you never had probably brings you great joy. Therein lies the conflict. How do you give your kids a good life without them feeling entitled to that good life?

How can you temper their incessant desire for things while encouraging them to live their "best life"? Shouldn't a little healthy desire for the good life give rise to ambition that could lay the foundation for financial success?

For me, I knew that traveling was a huge motivator when it came to taming my finances. With social media, I'm constantly served with images of people traveling and having fun while doing it. I both like and don't like it.

On the one hand, it makes we want to stick to my budget even more so I can travel more often. On the other hand, it ignites a desire in me to travel all the time!

You better believe that once we got out of debt, one of the first things we did was travel like crazy. And travel is still a big part of our lives now that our finances are under control.

While I don't want to squelch my daughter's desire for the nicer things in life because I think they can serve a purpose in helping them attain certain goals, I don't want to encourage entitlement and the spoiled suburbanite attitude that makes our young women think that they deserve everything in life.

So while this book is designed to help you have money conversations that will serve your kids for the rest of their lives, I think it's important also to have conversations that revolve around some of the issues you might be facing with your young girls right now—namely, those issues regarding money relations between parents and kids in the here and now.

I have a unique situation because my children actually earn money on their own already. As paid performers in the acting and entertainment industry, they've already begun amassing wealth at a young age. Fortunately, they have sizeable amounts of money in their savings and their brokerage accounts from these activities.

For this reason, my girls and I will have entirely different discussions around money in the here and now. Consequently, my husband and I are constantly balancing their desire for their money right away with the need to save for their future. It's a real issue and it has to be addressed on a daily basis in our home.

Though your daughters might not be earning money and/or have jobs right now, they still may get money in different ways. Perhaps they get money for their birthdays or money that comes in from relatives to celebrate milestones like graduation or getting good grades. More than likely, your kids get money in some form or another.

In some cases, you might think that the money they receive really is a little bit much. I mean what can a six-year-old do with $100? It is at this point that you're probably inclined to save that money up for her. At this stage, your six-year-old probably won't take issue with this decision.

But what do you do when your teenager is wondering why she can't spend the entire $150 that Grandma sent her for her birthday? That's a tough one. In fact, it's an issue that I deal with quite regularly. As my oldest daughter earns more money from her acting and voice-over jobs, she sees her checks and thinks that she's entitled to the entire amount.

Even though we've talked about how this money is better off in savings or invested in various types of stocks, she's been struggling with the idea of saving her money. I explain that we save so that when she is ready to go to college, get married, or even start having a family she could potentially have hundreds of thousands or even millions of dollars at her disposal. She's still learning about the time value of money, so it's been a difficult concept to grasp and believe.

We have this conversation regularly, yet she still wants to know why she can't use all of her money to buy all the clothes, all the electronic gadgets, and all the things that make her the "most beautiful girl in the world."

The struggle is very real, and your daughter won't stop asking for what she believes is due to her. So it's important that you have some decisions already made when it comes to how you'll handle money in the right here and now.

Though I don't have a hard-and-fast rule on how you should handle these money issues that will come up with your daughters, trying to anticipate them in advance should help you prepare.

Can I Have an Allowance?

This is perhaps one of my favorite topics to tackle when it comes to money and parenting. Your daughters may hear about their friends getting an allowance and wonder if this is something they can get as well.

I'm going to take a page from my favorite money guru, Dave Ramsey's book and say that your daughter shouldn't be entitled to an allowance unless she does something to earn it. In fact, there are a number of studies[1] proving that kids who go on to be successful adults typically had responsibilities like chores from a young age.

It might be tempting just to give your kids money for the sake of giving them money, but the best practice is to give them an allowance that is associated with work. Not only will this help them to develop a good work ethic, but also it will help them appreciate the value of money.

Many kids are shell-shocked in young adulthood as they enter into the real world without the slightest idea of how much life really costs. You can give your kids a glimpse into the world of working for money and then letting them use that money on their own needs.

Can I Use My Savings for XYZ?

This is a question that you'll always get when your kids find out that you've been saving up money for them. You might tell them

---

1   Albernaz, Ami. "Sparing Chores Spoils Children and Their Future Selves, Study Says." Boston Globe, December 8, 2015. https://www.bostonglobe.com/lifestyle/2015/12/08/research-indicates-sparing-chores-spoils-children-and-their-future-selves/ZLvMznpC5btmHtNRXXhNFJ/story.html.

that money is earmarked for college, or some other purpose beyond extreme needs for fast food, more clothes, and beauty stuff.

We'll talk about savings and savings goals a little bit later. But just know that it is okay to say yes and it is okay to say no to requests for money from savings.

Depending on the arrangement you set up with your daughter regarding her savings, your answer could vary and that's okay. You may find out you're dealing with an incredibly mature child who is able to replace the savings they want to deplete to go on a special trip or use to purchase their first car. You may also decide that there's just not enough wiggle room to chance withdrawing money that is supposed to be used for college or some other purpose.

I would say whatever answer you have, just be prepared to explain it and back it up with illustrations and logic (though these things are not always the average teen's forte.)

Then prepare to have that logic totally and utterly rejected. Because again, in many cases, we will be dealing with young women, and we all know that kids can be totally irrational at times. The good news is that you'll get to plant seeds as you have this conversation.

Even though your daughter might not get the money concept every time, she will probably always remember the conversation that she tried to have with you time and time again to take out money from her savings in order to buy XYZ.

She'll probably recount the story to her daughter saying how she felt and why she thought it was unfair and in that moment of retrospection and self-reflection she might understand why you made the decision that you did—whether you said yes or no.

Remember, as you have these conversations you may never totally convince your daughter of the most prudent thing to do with money—at first. Don't forget that planting seeds around wise money management is still a worthwhile endeavor. One day, they'll remember these money talks along with the lessons that came out of them.

Are We Poor? (How Much Money Do We Make?)

Depending on your family circumstances, your children may think that you are either incredibly rich or incredibly poor. The funny part is that you can be incredibly rich in assets and income but still live frugally enough for your kids to think that you're poor. That's not a bad thing!

If you get this question and that's exactly the case for your family, don't be shy about explaining what real wealth is. Feel free to explain to your daughters that outward appearances and materialistic *displays* of wealth don't always equate to wealth.

Conversely, if your daughters think that you have a never-ending supply of money but you struggle to pay the bills from month to month, it's still a good idea to be transparent in this way, too. It might feel embarrassing to admit that Mom and Dad have a spending problem, don't make enough money, or have a little bit too much credit card debt, but it's a way to start money conversations that could change your family tree for the better.

I think this question is best answered when you know how mature your child is, as well as her ability to grasp the concept of how much money your family brings in. It probably won't make much sense to tell your seven-year-old that Mommy and Daddy make a combined $250,000 per year. They may not have a good reference point to understand if that's a lot or a little money. The other option is to disclose the amount, then begin giving them references to wrap their minds around the number. You can say things like, "It costs $7,000 for a family trip to Disney" or "Our car costs $20,000." This way, they can understand what higher dollar amounts mean.

If you don't want to talk actual numbers yet, that's ok, too. When your daughter asks you this question, it might be good to counter with another question. This might help you understand why she wants to know details regarding your family's financial status.

Ask her, "Why are you asking about our finances?" or "What prompted you to ask this question?" She might say that her friend told her that her house was nice or some classmates called her out for having unfashionable shoes. She may even mention overhearing a conversation in the kitchen between her mom and dad worrying about how they would pay bills.

The motivation for the question might change the way you frame your answer. You may choose to quote a specific dollar amount or you may choose to use words that describe your financial situation.

You could use a combination of both explanations as needed. If you think your daughter might be concerned about the family having enough money, you can let her know that Mommy and Daddy make enough money but still need to do a better job at managing it.

You could explain that past decisions like student loans, car purchases, or opting for a big wedding still impacts your finances today. This would be a great time to explain how taking on debt can have an effect on your finances and quality of life well into the future.

If the question came about because your daughter feels shame for being better off than her peers, you can assure her along those lines as well. Firstly, you can let her know that Mommy and Daddy's money is just that. It belongs to you as the parents and technically she is not wealthy or affluent—yet—but it is okay to acknowledge that she comes from a wealthy or affluent family.

This is another teachable moment. Having a discussion about the responsibility that comes along with wealth and influence would be a perfect fit in this conversation. Encourage her to feel honored that she belongs to a family that has the potential to help others and do good in the world. It's also worth mentioning that just because Mom and Dad have money doesn't mean that she will inherently have the same status in life. Any inheritance or financial status that she hopes to attain later on in life will likely come from a combination of her own merits along with the inheritance. But the degree of both is dependent upon how she carries herself and how she demonstrates the maturity needed to steward that wealth. She should know that you expect her to use the resources she could be entrusted with in a way that will help society and others.

If you do feel like it's appropriate to throw an exact number out there, be prepared to discuss why you're able to make as much as you do. What kind of training or education got you to this place? What kind of goals and planning helped you achieved your status? Did you start with a smaller salary? If so, how long did it take for you to get to where you are?

Also, take this opportunity to explain where the money goes. When your daughter hears about all the money that you make, she might think you make a lot of money (or not enough.) It's okay to discuss the household expenses the family's income has to cover. It will help your daughter understand the true value of the money you earn and what it takes to live the lifestyle that she enjoys.

If there are any spending categories that you plan to adjust like eating out or leisure, it's totally fine to think aloud in her presence on how this spending can be improved. Again, one of the most valuable things you can do is show your daughter that you're open to changing the way that you do things with your money. Don't be afraid to *show* her and that you're still learning, even as an adult, how to do things better with your money.

If you feel like you're struggling with under-earning, talk about why that's the case as well. This conversation can be about how you plan to increase your earnings. This is another teachable moment that can impact your daughter for the better.

She can see, firsthand, that you are self-aware when it comes to your money problems and are taking responsibility to improve your personal financial situation. This is another great opportunity to think out loud while creating a game plan that can help you and your family reach your financial goals. This shows her that it's never too late and no one is ever too old to improve any situation in their life, including anything that pertains to finances.

Having Money Babies

This is a conversation that I have often with my daughters. We know that girls tend to be obsessive about their image and with those obsessions can come ungodly spending on fashion and beauty products.

These billion-dollar industries are largely fueled by young women who constantly struggle with self-esteem. They are hoping that their sense of self-worth will increase by improving the way they look, smell, etc. If we, as women, are not careful, this can be a huge drain on our pocketbooks, and our daughters will only follow suit!

As I mentioned, I feel like I'm in a never-ending battle with my teenager about saving her money to spend it on what matters. And it's not just my teenager. My preteen really likes to spend money on Barbies and Barbie's accessories. She even buys lots of craft items to make Barbie accessories.

To be clear, I don't expect my daughters to act like they are living in the Little House on the Prairie. It's not realistic to think that they will never spend any money and never desire anything. One thing I do drive home, almost on a daily basis, is the idea of using their money to buy things that can produce *more* money.

For example, my youngest daughter once asked me for more Barbies and Air Jordan shoes for her birthday. I purchased the stock for those companies that made those products instead.

She wasn't terribly excited, but I did explain to her that her Barbies and Air Jordans would not make her any money. I also told her that if she owned a little tiny piece of a company, that tiny piece could grow and grow and just as the company made millions and racked up profits, she could also partake in the company profits.

My oldest daughter is *always* asking me about getting some type of electronic. As you can imagine, these electronics are extremely expensive. For example, she's been asking about the latest iPhone, which costs about $1,000. Though she does have the money in her investing account to get it, I explained to her that we want that money to stay there and grow. Ideally, when she's older, she'll be able to use the profits earned on that money for something that could make even more money for her. That could be a college education, for example.

We also talk about how small amounts of money can be used to make what I call money babies. The key is that we have to take that money, put it away, and let it grow over an extended period of time. I try to explain that an iPhone today might be a multi-unit building forgone 20 years from now!

Don't get me wrong. More than likely, I will give in and let my daughter use some of her money to buy her iPhone. As of this writing, we have a deal that if she books a certain type of acting gig that can add more money to her bank account, then she'll be able to use some of that new money to purchase an iPhone. But I have to explain to her, over and over again, that we don't want to disturb money that we've "planted" in her savings and investments. We want it to be available so that it can grow to support her lifestyle down the road.

Growing up, I remember that my mother was very keen on getting us the latest and greatest in clothing, electronics, and grooming. If there was ever a time I wanted to get my hair done, there was nothing my mother wouldn't do to make sure that I could be well coiffed. It was important to her that I was dressed "to the nines" for any occasion. But as I said before, I sometimes wish that she would have withheld some of those things and instead put that money away in a bank account. I don't mean this to sound ungrateful, but I do realize that there are a lot of us as parents who do this very same thing.

This is what I mean. Whenever I have a niece, nephew, or a godchild, I tell the parent to open up this brokerage account and I will contribute money to purchase stocks or some other type of similar investment for your child.

And it is very interesting to me how many people don't take the offer! They will spend a lot of time with baby showers, birthday parties, prom send-offs, and lots of other fun things to give their child a good childhood experience. But when it comes down to doing something that could really make a difference in their children's lives financially, many people don't see the value. As a result, they don't even act on a free offer that could make their child a millionaire by the time he or she is 30 years old!

Having all the nice things as a child was great, and I thank my mother for it. However, I decided that I wanted my children's story to be different. As of this writing, if both of my children keep their "money babies" in the bank, they will easily hit millionaire status at some point in their life.

It will be up to them to steward the wealth and invest it wisely, however. I'm thankful we can also give our daughters things like experiences and nice clothing, but our priority has always been saving up money for their future and reinforcing wealth-building principles like business ownership and investing.

No, life does not have to be dull and all of our money invested in the stock market. But we do want to prioritize loving our future selves and making provision for the latter years of our lives as well. Again, I think that it's a conversation that can be worked into almost any experience or activity; you just have to be a little creative and definitely very intentional about it.

CHAPTER 6

Let's Talk Redefining Wealth

My daughters know that one of my triggers is when people equate wealth and affluence with someone's outward appearance. If one of them makes a comment about someone else's nice car or nice clothes sometimes they'll follow it up with, "They must be making a lot of money."

In some cases, that is true. There are people that can truly afford nice things because they have the money to purchase them. But I do try to offer another perspective that could also be true—some people are "faking the funk." (Explanation to follow.)

This is a conversation that I have with my daughters constantly. Though I don't get down on them about desiring nice things or admiring people who have nice things, I do try to provide an additional point of view. It is my hope that this view will keep them grounded and will dictate how they view and define wealth for themselves in the coming years. One thing that I want to separate is the idea that just because someone has nice things or makes a lot of money means that they are rich.

Even the person that earns and seems to have a lot of money to buy those things may still be living paycheck-to-paycheck. There are plenty of statistics and stories on the web that talk about the phenomenon of the upper middle class struggling and just being a couple of paychecks from total financial disaster.

Yes, even that doctor who seems to be the richest person you'll ever meet could be struggling to juggle student loan payments, a large mortgage, private school tuition for several kids, and a host of other expenses that can overtake high earners.

One thing that separates Americans from the rest of the world is that higher income gives us easier access to credit. As it were, it becomes pretty easy to "present" as a wealthy person simply by being able to make low monthly payments on our belongings. This is what I call "faking the funk."

When we see people who seem to be living their best lives, it can make us think that someone has it all together when they don't. It's easy—especially in the social media age—for us to look at someone and assume that they must have a lot of money. They could be experiencing inordinate amounts of stress because of their financial indiscretions. There could be crippling anxiety keeping them from functioning because they fear never having enough money. That person may owe more money to their creditors than they can afford to pay. There are so many possibilities beyond what we see. For this reason, we should not assume that anyone is better off than they are or feel shame when it looks like someone else has more than we have.

If we are tempted to compare and judge someone who seems to be wealthy, we can analyze what can be going on. (For our own sanity, at least.)

A few things could be going on when we see people with lots of nice things. For one, they may place high value on having nice things. They may also place low value on saving money for assets that enable them to make more money.

Now, I don't want to ever give my daughters the idea that being a good saver and having nice things are mutually exclusive mindsets. That's not always the case. But I do want to paint a picture that gives all the possibilities to someone looking in from the outside wondering why their lives might not measure up to the seemingly financially secure people they encounter.

Another possibility is that someone could have inherited a substantial amount of money. The money they inherited may have come to them easily. It's for this reason that they can drop a few thousand dollars on a nice designer bag.

One other possibility is that they actually work hard, earn a lot of money, and they just like nice things. They could also have a sizeable savings account. Even in these situations, we should not feel bad about seeing someone or hearing about their success and comparing ourselves.

Wealth should not be measured by the number of physical objects someone possesses. True wealth is knowing what we value in our lives and being able to attain it. It could include looking wealthy, actually being wealthy, or both.

We've all heard stories about celebrities that have to file bankruptcy and even those that have been in prison for financial crimes like tax evasion. *Broke*, a famous documentary on ESPN from 2012, profiled a number of NBA and NFL athletes who were broke just a few years after retiring from their professional sports career. Even though they had made millions of dollars, they didn't know how to manage their money so that it didn't evaporate into thin air.

We know that it's possible that even the high-earners among us can be struggling even though there is an outward display of wealth in the form of fancy cars, large houses, and all the accoutrement of high-end living.

Thus, the question becomes how will we guide our daughters as they try to define wealth for themselves? We can do that when we define what our wealthy place looks like.

For me, true wealth is having more than enough to accommodate my family's needs but also be able to help others accomplish their God-given purpose in life.

Wealth for me is being able to travel, go on mission trips, and have a career where I can help people establish financial foundations that enable them to accomplish what they've been called to. Wealth is being able to sit down and have conversations like this with my daughters even in my imperfect financial state.

Having money conversations with our daughters is about defining what wealth looks like for ourselves and then letting our daughters do the same. You might be a person that values a large comfortable home and beautiful luxury cars. Conversely, you might be a person that would take a smaller home for the opportunity to travel around the world.

How you define wealth for yourself is a very personal endeavor and it will mean the world to your daughters' pursuit of wealth and happiness, too. I think it's important to personalize this definition because if we let someone else's definition of a rich life define us we will ultimately be striving for the wrong things. We don't want our daughters following that path; we want to teach them to blaze their own.

CHAPTER 7

Let's Talk Dreams and Goals

When it's time to start talking about money with your daughters I find that the best way to frame the conversation is really, "How do you want your life to look?" It's from this place that my girls get excited.

If you start from dreaming about the future and all its exciting possibilities, you'll likely get a better response from your young ones—especially with teenagers. They are so finicky that you might have to finesse some things out of them by reframing the conversation to be all about them and what they want.

Girls get giddy with excitement when you ask them about their future. They can tell you the type of person they want to marry, what the wedding will be like, where they'll live, and the profession in which they see themselves. Some will even go so far as to tell you about the number of children and grandchildren they'll have.

When you start off like this, you can also take time to discuss how you thought *your* future would pan out. It might seem a little painful to bring up dreams you feel never got fulfilled, but it's still a good exercise. It allows you to reflect on where your teenage brain was when you had these thoughts about the future.

You may even find that you are doing almost exactly what you envisioned you would do or perhaps you're doing something very close to it. You may discover that the future you envisioned for yourself isn't that far away and there's still a lot more time to realize the dreams you had as a youngster.

As you verbalize these thoughts, your daughter might see some similarities and her own hopes for the future and realize what it takes for these dreams to materialize. More often than not, young women will envision a future that is pretty grandiose and outlandish by any stretch of the imagination. Personally, I think that's the way it should be and that we should encourage our daughters to dream even bigger.

The mystery ingredient is what it actually takes for those dreams to become a reality. As young women, we think that whatever fantasy we've created for the future will automatically come to pass when, in reality, we've got to be ready to take the steps on the path to that dream life.

If we imagine ourselves living a life where we can do whatever we want whenever we'd like to do it (because let's face it, that's what all of our fantasy lives boil down to), then we've got to prepare for that reality. That preparation entails being financially secure in some form or another.

Financial security doesn't have to be piles of money in the bank or reaching millionaire status or being counted among the wealthiest people in the world. As long as you get to live the quality of life you desire, you can consider yourself financially secure.

For some people, financial security might look like living a scaled-down version of life in a low-cost-of-living country. You may not have a lot of money to your name but where you live and the kind of life you've created for yourself doesn't require much money. In this case, you do have financial security.

For others, financial security means having a sizable nest egg and it's definitely needed for a high quality of life in retirement. If you plan to retire on a tropical island with a beach house (pool included) with servants to help run your household, then yes, your flavor of financial security will look different than that of the next person.

No matter what financial security means for you, you still need to make a plan to get there. So when you start the conversation about money matters with your daughters, make sure you let them know that whatever they desire is possible. They'll just have to prepare for it.

For some young women that may definitely mean millionaire status and for others it may mean crafting a life that works within the money they already have—perhaps based on their chosen profession or the amount of income earned related to that profession.

Rather than focusing on money, it's a good idea to start with a purpose that can be expressed as a personal mission and vision statement. These concepts might seem a little abstract in the beginning, but you can help your daughter arrive at her vision and mission with some of the following prompts:

- What does the perfect day look like for you?
- What excites you?
- What kind of work would you do, if no one paid you?
- What do you want to be remembered for?
- If you could do anything with your day, all day, what would it be?
- What do you think you'll be doing when you turn 20? 30? 40?
- What do you think your biggest contribution to the world will be?
- What kind of money do you think it will take to live the life you want to live?
- How much money do you think you will need in the bank to do _____?
- What kind of profession or career or business could you start to get that kind of money?
- What kind of education or training will it take to enter your dream field?
- How much money will your education and training cost?

Once this is done, you might be able to better guide them toward a personal vision and mission statement. A vision statement is how the ideal life looks while a mission statement expresses how the outcome or vision will be achieved.

Here are some examples:

- My vision is to make the world a better place by
  _____.
- My vision is to help people achieve _____.
- My mission is to empower people to _____.

Dreaming is fun. Casting the possibilities the future may hold is exciting. This is exactly why I encourage you to start from this place and let the money conversations flow from this perspective.

Remember, as your daughters share these intimate hopes with you, make sure you are in listening mode. Try to suspend your judgment if their assumptions about life and the way the world works seem slightly askew.

It's quite possible that they'll change their answers to the questions quite often. And that's okay; as they talk things out they get to process them as well. Your role is to help them verbalize their dreams and hopes. You can certainly provide direction and realistic expectations as needed, but try mostly to help them "birth" these delicate hopes and dreams lying dormant inside of them.

As much as possible, encourage them and let them know that anything is possible (within reason) and if, alas, their expectations seem impossible, ask gentle nonjudgmental questions to help get them on the right track.

You can probably already imagine that your moody, hormonal teenager would love to spite you by answering some of these questions in the weirdest ways. Remain unbothered!

For example, your teen daughter might tell you, "I just want to eat all day and be a millionaire." This may or may not be true. But let's suppose that on a subconscious level it really represents something they'd like to do. You can redirect the conversation and tell them something along the lines of, "You know there are a lot of food shows and influencers who actually get paid to try new foods all around the world. What if you studied broadcast journalism and became an on-screen talent for a show like that?"

You could also bring the dream closer to reality, "Hey, what if you became a YouTuber that went around the city tasting different foods at different food spots? That's something you can do right now!"

As you can see, even if what your kids are saying to you seems like pie-in-the-sky pipe dreams, there might be truths that you can draw out of their seemingly unrealistic goals for their life.

Again, the goal is to listen, be nonjudgmental, and provide guidance as much as you can.

For kids, it can be quite hard to get them to start thinking seriously about their future. Don't let that deter you either. My daughters have been known to goof off and act like they're not all that interested in the conversation. When this happens, I drop the conversation and plan to pick it up at another time when they are feeling more chatty or less combative.

Another activity that can be helpful with this conversation is creating vision boards. Kids, girls especially, tend to like arts and crafts. Give them some magazines, color pencils, and glue sticks and you've got a party. If they don't want to talk about their future and their dreams they might be more inclined to put them on a poster board and color it with crayons. Do whatever it takes!

I've done this activity several times with my daughters and they seem to like it. With the vision board activity, I'm able to figure out what motivates them and what they think their future will look like. Strangely enough, I can say that many of the things my daughters have put on their vision boards and subsequently talked about have already come to pass! It's a powerful activity that can help your daughters figure out what they want their lives to look like.

The point here is to show your daughters that they can create their own story and make their own happy ending. When you're able to talk about their future or put it on a vision board they start to see and believe that this is true.

CHAPTER 8

Let's Talk Plans and Actions

Now that you've helped your daughters dream, it's time to help them take action. The vision they have for the future, when expressed in conversation or writing, should start to subconsciously program them to work toward that future.

There are a couple of ways you can have these conversations about how to act on their dreams. They can be informal—just infused in your everyday interactions with your daughters. There are lots of teachable moments to be had when they are talking about their day or just observing the world around them. The benefit of this approach is that you can make money talk naturally a part of your regular activities. It also gives you a lot of practice talking about money with your daughters.

The other approach is to schedule money chats. I have a recurring appointment on my calendar to talk with my daughters about their savings and other money conversations. Though we don't always make the appointment (life happens, right?), it's good to know that we've carved out some time to at least talk about it.

I think it's a good idea to do a combination of each approach. It will give you an idea of what works best for your money chats and help you stay consistent once you find an approach that you like.

Planning for the Vision

In the beginning, you don't have to attach a dollar amount to the dreams and goals, but it will be necessary at some point. Right now, you'll just want to break apart each detail of what your daughter desires for her "dream life." Eventually, you'll work together to map out what it takes to get there.

For example, if going to college is part of the picture, then you'll want to write out basic things that need to happen like:

- Taking college prep classes
- Maintaining a _____ GPA
- Getting a _____ on ACTs/SATs
- Choosing a major or career focus
- Choosing a desired college
- Completing FAFSA forms
- Completing scholarship forms
- Excelling at _____ sport

If your daughter looks beyond college, she might have additional goals like starting a family or running a business. Those lists could look like this:

- Get an internship with _____ company
- Create a savings account to buy/start business in related industry
- Get certified in _____
- Take exam for _____

Other life events to consider include:

- Buying a home
- Getting married
- Having a child
- Retirement

While it might be tempting to focus on the far out, big goals, don't forget to include smaller more immediate goals like buying a car or attending a special summer camp. This is especially important because you want to give your girls the opportunity to build confidence with small wins. If they don't have experience winning with smaller things, it will be difficult for them to believe that they're able to attain much larger goals.

Once you get a list of short-term and long-term life goals in place with your daughters, along with the steps it will take to bring these goals to fruition, it's time to talk about money. Each one of these goals along with the action steps will require some type of resource. For some goals, it may simply mean there is a time commitment involved. For other goals, money will definitely need to be in place.

Now would be a great time to bring your daughter back to earth with some realistic figures and what it takes to accomplish things like attending college, going to a special summer camp, or even purchasing her first car.

Let's take the goal of purchasing a car, since many of you will have daughters who are closer to that milestone than any other you'll discuss. Now, if your daughters are anything like I was when I was growing up, I simply thought that having a car meant I get to park my butt behind a steering wheel and ride around with a car full of friends.

I didn't think anything about how much the car cost, what it would take to maintain it, or even any insurance requirements. I just thought that getting a car meant . . . just that—getting one.

For the sake of being super clear and explicit, write down the total cost of owning a car for your daughter and let her see the numbers for herself:

- Driver education course—$150–$200
- Driver's license—$30–$50
- Cost of car—$3,000 to $5,000 (you may choose to finance a car, so this might be a monthly figure)

- Insurance—$100–$150 per month
- Maintenance—$50–$100 per month
- Auto fuel—$50–$75 per month

Once you attach these numbers to what it takes to own and operate a car, your daughter will start to see what a big commitment it is. Now, how you handle these expenses will be up to you.

For us, there are some expenses that we pay for our daughters and others we make them pay for. You know your child and the level of responsibility she needs to develop along with how likely they are to work to maintain their driving privileges. Based on all this information, you should come up with an arrangement that works for you and your family.

I highly advise against just covering everything for them. After all, if they never have to pay for anything they use, they could abuse their privileges or not appreciate what you're doing for them. When it's time for them to cover their own expenses in the real world, the adjustment of paying for everything could be extremely difficult for them.

Now, you might see this and be shocked that the cost of car ownership is so high and there's no way a teenager could possibly cover that. I would suggest starting off with an even smaller goal. For example, my fourteen-year-old daughter covers half of her $30 phone bill each month.

When it's time for her to drive, we will discuss all of the costs and then work out a plan to split them with her accordingly. Another option would be to allow your child to drive the family car but still be responsible for covering their insurance and fuel costs. This might be ideal if you don't anticipate purchasing another car for your teenager.

Again, there are lots of ways to skin a cat here. The goal is really just to have a discussion so that your daughters know you are not trying to put a huge burden on them with these expenses. Rather, you are trying to help them navigate the real world of expenses in a way that they are not overwhelmed while also making them responsible and realistic with money.

The same conversation can be had about college expenses. The sooner you discuss how everything will work regarding college tuition, the sooner your daughters can begin to set their expectations on how these expenses will be covered.

Letting them know on the eve of their 16th birthday that they won't be getting a car is definitely a bad idea—especially if you know they've been making plans on this outcome for quite some time. Technically, these are your kids and you really don't owe them an explanation of your plans, but I still think it's courteous to at least involve them in the conversation so they can make other plans if their expectations are not met. Having a productive, respectful conversation, even when they are disappointing, can help your daughters mature in ways you could never have imagined.

The same can go for college, paying for your daughter's wedding, or even helping to cover her first home. Your daughter will have many influences outside of your home and will observe how many of her peers' families handle expenses related to milestones. If Katie's mom and dad pay for her car, college tuition, and wedding, your daughter might think she has the same thing coming. And why should she not? In order to avoid any confusion, it's best to have these conversations and set expectations as soon as possible.

CHAPTER 9

Let's Talk Budgeting

No matter how young your daughter is, she's never too young to learn about the concept of budgeting. Budgeting isn't all about numbers and how they add up or take away from your money supply. The concept of budgeting simply demonstrates that money is a finite resource and that it must be managed according to what is available.

Of course you won't pull up a spreadsheet with your six-year-old and go through the budget, line by line, but you can convey the idea of managing a limited money supply. You can start to communicate with her about how you allocate your money according to your financial goals.

I began to teach my daughters about the concept of budgeting before they could even do math very well. We'd be at the grocery store and they'd ask, "Mommy, can we buy this bag of candy?" or "Mommy, can we get this type of cereal?" And because we were in the process of paying down debt, I was very motivated to stick firmly to our grocery budget.

Instead of telling my daughters, "No, we don't have the money," I would tell them I didn't bring money for that, and that the money I have is available for XYZ.

Even though they didn't always like this answer, it began to train their mind according to a budget mentality. When we communicate to our children that, yes, money is available but has another assignment aside from buying candy or cereal, we are giving them a preview of what it means to plan how our money is used—aka budgeting

When we bring up budgeting in this way, it does a couple of things. Number one, it builds trust with our kids. To tell our kids that we don't have money when we do is dishonest. Of course, there are times when you can truly say you don't have any money, but how many times have you said that to your kids in the store and it wasn't true?

I'm a big fan of using words to say what they mean and mean what they say. I need my words to work powerfully on my behalf to create the kind of existence that I desire for myself. So I am very conscientious about using the right words. You should be too.

Number two, telling your daughters that there is money available affirms the idea that money, though finite in nature, is available in abundance if the proper steps are taken to access it.

Now that you've been particular with your words and you've introduced some abstract concepts like the finite nature of money, at some point you will have to introduce more practical ways to manage it. This conversation can seem difficult to have if you're not one to deal with numbers. When it comes to mixing math and children, people tend to get anxious.

While I don't want to add to your anxiety, I do think that you should make the effort to get comfortable around using simple addition and subtraction with your daughter to teach her about managing her money. It's a powerful concept that someone with a first grade math level is able to budget. That's really all it comes down to—addition and subtraction. If you and your daughters can do that, you all are already prepared to have a concrete practical discussion about budgeting.

I think a great time to have this conversation is right after you talk about dreams and goals. After this conversation, your daughters will be excited, hopeful, and looking forward to having their dream life come true. It's at this point that you should feel comfortable talking about the tools that can lay the foundation for those dreams and goals to come to pass.

I remember being young and fantasizing about all the nice things that I would have and all the money I would spend on those nice things. But wouldn't you know it, I never could come up with a solid plan regarding the income I'd earn to get all of those things.

Sure, I knew how to dream, make goals, and speculate about the millions that I would make as soon as I moved out of my mother's home, but I wasn't taught about the different tools that could help me live the kind of lifestyle that I had always wanted to live.

Again, this conversation is not about you being perfect with money. In fact, it may go over better if you're able to share many of the mistakes and misfortunes you had with money. Perhaps one of the biggest regrets that many people have is that all the money that flowed through their hands never had purpose or direction.

The one way to make sure that money is funneled where it belongs is by creating a budget. A budget may sound restrictive, but it's really no more than a spending plan that gives you freedom. It helps to put your money where your financial goals are met.

I heard one person put it this way, "You can do anything, but you just can't do everything." In other words, you can do whatever you set your mind to but at the end of the day, there are limitations to resources like energy and money. But you can budget those resources in order to get the outcomes you are seeking in life.

For example, I'm a person who really enjoys traveling. I'm willing to forgo some things like frequent purchases of nice purses and nice shoes in order to make room for travel. I'd also happily restrict these purchases for business opportunities that could bring in additional income. This extra income could also help afford more travel.

Conversely, you might be someone who is totally opposite, and perhaps travel isn't your cup of tea. No matter what your "thing" is, the objective is to put your money in places that help you reach your financial goals. The way to do this is through budgeting.

A budget tells your money where to go every month instead of wondering where it went. You can be proactive and tell your money, "Hey money, this is what we're going to do this month." That's all a budget is.

Also, it's good to discuss that there are different ways to budget. I personally am really into spreadsheets, so creating a budget is helpful for me. But then, there are others who aren't into spreadsheets and prefer to break their budget down into percentages or buckets. A common way to use the percentage buckets is using the 50-30-20 rule:

- 50 percent toward necessities like housing and bills
- 30 percent toward wants like travel, entertainment, and dining out
- 20 percent toward financial goals like paying down debt and saving for retirement

You can also choose to adjust these categories as you see fit. Some options include trying to decrease your overall cost of living or putting more toward debt repayment. For us, we decided early on that we would tackle one of our largest expenses: our living expense. When we first got married, we rented a tiny apartment for about $700 a month.

Then we moved to a larger home that we rented for $1,400 a month, but a relative moved in with us and we split the rent with them. After that, we were fortunate to live with my mother, who was kind enough not to charge us rent. It was during this time that we were able to pay off tons of debt and eventually save enough money to move into another home.

As I mentioned in our money story, relatives who had inherited a home but didn't want to live in the inner city subsequently offered us their home. We took it because it was mortgage-free and rent-free. Because of that move, we were able to pay off more than $120,000 in consumer debt.

To this day, we have very few expenses when it comes to our room and board. We do have a small mortgage on an investment property that will be paid off very soon. Having a low cost of living has enabled us to pay off debt, increase our savings, and take off some of the pressure of needing two incomes to support our household. For this opportunity I'm thankful.

I realize that everyone may not have the luxury of moving in with a relative and then receiving a home without a mortgage or having to pay rent. I strongly believe that we all face some sort of advantage, and it's up to us to identify these opportunities and capitalize on them.

Even if you are a grown woman reading this, you may have the opportunity to take on a roommate or move back in with a relative. Maybe you can't get a roommate or move in with someone, but perhaps you can share other expenses, like splitting wi-fi with a neighboring tenant or subscription services with a friend or family member.

There are many options when it comes to decreasing your living expenses, but we'll cover those in another chapter. Here, we want to simply give our daughters ideas about being frugal so that you can arrive at a budget split that works for you.

There are infinite variations in the percentage budget that will work for you and your money priorities. The important thing is that you create budget categories that help you reach your financial goals.

With that said, the budget is a spending plan that only works when you set caps on your spending and you adhere to them. If you're familiar with the Dave Ramsey method of paying off debt, then you might have heard of something called a cash envelope. To me, this is one of the best ways to set spending boundaries that correspond to a spending plan.

For example, if you set spending boundaries in the area of groceries, eating out, and entertainment, you'll want to have cash envelopes for those categories. When you get paid, you'll pay all of the bills that you budgeted for online and then pull out the rest of the cash to fill your envelopes for those categories.

If your grocery budget is $400 for the month, you'll put $400 into your grocery envelope. If your entertainment budget is $100 per month, you'll put $100 in that envelope. When the money is gone from the envelopes, that means there's no more to spend in that budget category. This system worked pretty well for our family until we paid the last of our debt.

However, I do realize that it can be difficult to solely depend on cash. If you are someone that uses a lot of digital platforms and apps to conduct business, it might be hard to use cash. For example, if you're someone who relies on Uber or Lyft to get around, of course you can't set your transportation budget with cash. You'll have to use a debit or credit card.

When I work with people who have this type of situation (meaning that cash isn't that convenient for them) I suggest a "digital envelope system." You can create digital envelopes by opening multiple bank accounts that correspond to your budget categories.

The best way to do this is with an online bank. You can certainly go to a brick and mortar bank but it could have higher fees and charge you to open several accounts.

If you are the person who wants to put limits on the transportation budget category, then you'd create an online account and give it an account nickname of transportation. Once you are issued a debit card for this account, place a small sticker with the word "transportation" on it; anytime you get a bus card, catch a Lyft, or rent a bicycle, this will be the card used to cover those expenses.

So when you're shopping for a bank account to help you accomplish this type of digital envelope system, look for ones that:

- Allow you to open multiple checking accounts (savings, too) with no fees
- Allow you to give accounts nicknames
- Will issue debit cards for your checking accounts
- Have an easy-to-use app so you can check balances

Budgeting is a skill that can take time to master. Chances are the first time that you or your daughter create a budget, it will be pretty inaccurate. Why? Well, the simple answer is that we tend to forget many of our expenses that come up regularly and especially those that come up irregularly.

Expenses like property taxes or your car insurance that you pay every six months can be easy to forget about. It's likely that you will create a budget and keep drafting and revising it until it can be as accurate as possible. The idea is to forecast our expenses and plan out where every dollar will go that comes into our possession.

Again, you might be thinking, "Jeesh, I've always been bad with money and I've never created a budget. How can I have this conversation with my daughter if it's something I've never done myself?"

If that's the case, just share that with your daughter. It can be helpful to share your desire to start budgeting. Who knows? Maybe you can learn together.

If your daughter is still in grade school or high school and you think she doesn't have a lot of money to deal with, you'd be surprised at how much money you "give" her to cover many of her basic needs. For example, when you go out to eat you might be used to mindlessly swiping your debit or credit card to cover the entire bill.

We started giving our daughters an allowance so that when we go out to eat they can actually cover their own food. Even though it's from money that I gave them as an allowance, it gives them the chance to practice budgeting and making small money decisions. When they begin to drive, they will cover a portion of their car insurance and gas.

If it's possible, go into your spending report and see how much you're giving your kids for basic necessities. Then, begin funneling some of that money through *their* hands. You want them to understand how money works so they can begin making their own tiny budgeting decisions right now. Hopefully, once they move out on their own or go away to college, they will have had enough practice with managing their money that it won't be overwhelming for them.

And if you still feel very incompetent when it comes to budgeting and making good money decisions, just know that you don't have to do it on your own. It can be as simple as going to YouTube, home of thousands of personal finance YouTubers who will gladly show you how to create a budget and how to stick with it.

The budgeting system that we followed was from Dave Ramsey's *The Total Money Makeover* book. If he's not your cup of tea, there are plenty of other books, resources, and spreadsheet templates that you can reference to learn how to create and stick to a budget.

Remember, budgeting and money management are skills that can take time to develop. But if you stick with them, it'll show your daughter tenacity and willingness to learn money concepts.

CHAPTER 10

Let's Talk Saving

Saving is one of my very favorite topics. As a recovering shopaholic and money "mismanager," saving money was always difficult and proved very elusive for me. As I mentioned before I was a great worker bee, but I didn't know how to save what I earned.

When I turned 13 or 14 years old, I began to make money babysitting. At the age of 15, I got a job stuffing coleslaw into little cups. By the time I was legally allowed to work at 16, I already had two to three jobs under my belt in about a year's time.

I loved to work and make money, but I had no idea what to do when it came to putting my money away and saving. I had a checking account and I knew how to suck that thing dry with all my consumerism and spendthrift ways.

But saving? I thought that I didn't make enough money or that I would never have enough money to put away and save it. As someone once said, "It's not how much money you make; it's how much money you save."

If you feel too ashamed to have this conversation with your daughter because you yourself are not a great saver, don't feel bad. Americans are chronic undersavers. According to a shocking survey by Bankrate from 2016, almost 63 percent of Americans don't have enough savings to cover a $500 emergency.[1]

The likely culprit is the culture in which we live. We are bombarded with images of the beautiful lifestyles of the rich and famous almost daily. In fact, we probably see it more often because of social media.

What's more is that many of the beautiful lifestyle influencer blogger types we see seem to be people just like us. If they are living well and "high on the hog," why can't we? And so continues the cycle of vicious consumerism and chronic undersaving.

When I talk to my friends about saving, they give a lot of reasons (many of which I've had myself) for why they don't save money. Some of those reasons include:

- Not seeing a true need to save (people tend to depend on credit cards for emergencies)
- Not making enough money to save on a consistent basis
- Having high expenses which prevents saving
- Not having a good system in place to make sure that saving is a priority

There are so many reasons to save money, but the biggest one is to ensure that you don't go into debt covering emergencies and unexpected expenses. When you go into debt, you are also robbing yourself of the ability to save money due to paying interest on debt.

I've always said, "One thing about unexpected expenses is that they'll always come up. So it's best to just plan for them." One month, your kid might need a new pair of shoes and another month it could

---

1   McGrath, Maggie. "63% Of Americans Don't Have Enough Savings To Cover A $500 Emergency." Forbes. Forbes, January 6, 2016. https://www.forbes.com /sites/maggiemcgrath/2016/01/06/63-of-americans-dont-have-enough-savings -to-cover-a-500-emergency/#6eed0d074e0d.

be a house fire that requires a $1,000 deductible payment to your homeowners insurance.

Unexpected expenses will come up in some form or another almost every month. You don't know how they'll come; you just know they'll come.

But let's talk about how a lack of saving can create a vicious cycle of debt and undersaving. For example, let's say that you need some work done on your car. If you've got savings to cover it all, you won't need to use a credit card, which will charge you high interest rates on all purchases—big and small. Your $200 brake job could end up costing you $400 or $600 dollars by the time you've paid off the credit card balance.

Money paid on interest is money that could be saved for more of what you like to do. After all, who wants to pay double, triple, or quadruple for the basic necessities of life? I'm sure you don't. That's why it's essential to cultivate a habit of saving money no matter what.

Here's why you should earn interest instead of paying it. Banks will give you a measly 1 to 2 percent on your savings deposits, then turn around and give you a credit card where they will charge you anywhere from 15 to 30 percent or even more in interest. What a spread! It's equivalent to highway robbery. But many consumers willingly enter into credit card agreements without batting an eye.

When you look at it that way, it should motivate you to earn interest instead of paying interest. Unless you are a saver and investor, you will not earn interest on your hard-earned money. If you decide to remain a consumer that depends on debt to finance your lifestyle, you'll pretty much always be behind and making the banks rich by paying ridiculous amounts of interest.

I think the conversation that you'll have around saving money will be one of the most critical conversations that you can have with your daughters. When you demonstrate the act of saving money for yourself, you are demonstrating a form of self-love. In a world where women are made to be objects of self-loathing and disrespect, one of the most precious gifts you can give your daughter is the ability to love herself.

Saving money for your future is an act of love for both your present self and future self. For your present self, you are choosing to practice discipline and self-control, which will serve a greater good in your life. For your future self, your belief that you are worth the time and energy it takes to develop a consistent saving habit will benefit you in the future.

You can advise your daughters that, although women are encouraged to be selfless and nurturing, saving money is an act of self-preservation. When you save money, you're saying to yourself, "I hold the power to control my future and my destiny."

As a consistent saver, you develop an amazing confidence around your ability to exercise self-control and good money management. As mentioned in chapter 3, most women discount their ability to manage money because they lack confidence.

Developing a saving habit is perhaps one of the simplest things you can do to show up for yourself and develop confidence with financial decisions.

Yes, putting away just $5 a week can build an amazing amount of confidence that carries over into your professional career, love life, and other critical areas of life. Once you figure out that you can first show up for yourself, showing up for everyone, including your daughter, becomes that much easier.

Just like budgeting or any other money practice, it's never too late to start saving money. When you talk about saving (or your lack thereof) with your daughter, don't be shy about where you messed up and what you could have done better. They will appreciate the transparency and enjoy seeing you start your own consistent saving habit.

Now that we understand how important it is to save to avoid going into debt and for demonstrating self-love, it's also important that we talk about how saving can help you with your future.

For example, you may decide that you just can't give one more ounce of energy to your nine-to-five job. You really feel a tugging on your heart to start your own business. That decision is so much easier to make if you've got a savings cushion.

Maybe you don't want to start a business. You might just want a sabbatical or hiatus from work just because. Mental health breaks are totally valid reasons to take that time off from work.

If this is the case, your extended break may not come with paid time off. However, you'll still have expenses to take care of. This is another thing that is much easier to do if you've got some money saved.

There are plenty of reasons to save. A savings cushion can save your sanity and be there when you need it most. At the end of the day, having money saved up even in small amounts can provide such a peace of mind to help you get through life with the least amount of stress possible.

So as you start the savings conversation, be honest about where you are within your own savings journey and what you have yet to accomplish. When it's time to talk to your daughters about saving, make sure that you bring up points about avoiding debt, leaving the consumerism life behind, and creating a financial cushion for the future. Remind them that ensuring peace of mind through adequate savings demonstrates one of the highest forms of self-love.

How Can I Teach My Daughters to Become Savers?

The best way to teach your daughters to become savers is to become one yourself. There are so many strategies that you can use to become a professional saver that it should not be hard for you to find a method that works.

Be sure to explore different methods and talk about how they work with your daughters' personalities. It doesn't necessarily matter the method they choose to employ, just that they are saving sooner than later.

Savings Goals

There are a couple of ways that you can set up savings goals. You can look at different methods and see which one works best for your circumstances. One way you can do it is by setting an overarching savings goal. You can simply say to yourself that I want to save X percent of my income.

Once you set a savings goal, you can put it in a savings account that acts as a catchall for all of your savings needs. This can be especially helpful when you're talking with your daughters who may not have the burden of a bunch of expenses or the luxury of a regular paycheck.

Then, you can set specific savings goals for certain events or expenses. Why? Well, when you talk about saving money, it can be a little abstract and honestly demotivating to talk about money just for the sake of saving money. Your daughter might not think that it's fun just to have money sitting around that does nothing for her.

In this case, it would be a good idea for them to create savings goals. Since you've gone through the dreams and goals chapter with your daughter, you should have a lot of examples of savings goals that she can set right away.

Let her be creative. Perhaps she wants to get a new tennis racquet or to begin putting money away for her share of car expenses so she can be ready to drive. As soon as your daughter expresses a desire to accomplish some goal, you can create a savings account to put money toward that goal.

With this approach, you are working as a team. You are released from the burden of trying to provide every single thing your daughter needs, and she now has the responsibility of making things happen for herself (with some help from Mom).

Some goals are just so far away that it wouldn't make sense for your nine- or ten-year-old to start saving for them now. One example might be her wedding. You can create a savings timeline of sorts that indicates though saving for a wedding is too early right now, by this date you should begin saving. (You can, however, start investing for things like this on your daughter's behalf, but we'll cover that approach in the next chapter).

This will at least subconsciously put it on the radar of your daughter so that when she gets closer to the age when she could get married, she can create a related savings goal and savings account to get started on that goal.

Once savings goals are established, it's relatively easy to open a bank account, whether it's for a minor or for an adult. For some banks, you can even create several types of savings accounts and give them nicknames so you know exactly what each type of savings is for.

Decreasing Expenses to Save More

I've talked about this a couple of times, but it bears repeating in the savings discussion. One way that we started taking control of our finances was by simply decreasing our expenses. At the time, we really didn't have a lot of money smarts or confidence in our money-managing abilities. The lowest hanging fruit was to be as frugal as possible. That approached worked well until we were able to increase our income.

Now, there is somewhat of a debate that goes on in the personal finance community around cutting expenses to get ahead financially. This is known as the latte factor. It's really a way to show how the little, everyday expenses affect your ability to become financially stable.

It's like death by a thousand cuts—the small habits that add up to make a big impact on your budget. Think about going drinking on the weekends and having a daily latte. These seemingly small treats can impact your financial outcome in a negative way.

There are some people who say if you enjoy lattes, gosh-darn-it get a latte and get it every day. The latte is not going to make or break your finances. Then, there are those that say well if you add up the cost of a $5 latte over the course of a year you're spending something like $1,500 to $2,000 per year, which if you saved up over 30 years and compounded at the rate of 9 percent, would give you something like a million trillion dollars (I'm exaggerating of course; the real amount would be something like $270,000).

Using the investing calculator at investor.gov, here's how the math works out:

- $5 latte over 365 days a year would cost roughly $1,825 a year
- You'll invest $1,825 per year (or $152.08 per month) in the stock market for 30 years
- At a 9 percent yield, you'd have $248,755.81 at the end of 30 years
- At a 4 percent yield, you'd have $102,352.77 at the end of 30 years

The funny thing is that the people who tell you how to get that million or trillion dollars never have that million trillion dollars themselves. So I'd like to present a more balanced, practical approach.

Examine your latte factor and cut out what you can. If you have some expenses that give you peace of mind, by all means, keep them or try to keep them in a way that they don't affect your ability to become a saver.

For example, if you have a habit of going to the salon twice a month and getting your nails done three times a month, maybe cut back to one to two visits per month total. You may choose to cut more, but at least start someplace.

The rate at which you are willing to cut expenses is known by the Dave Ramsey Community as "gazelle intensity." In other words, how willing are you to reduce your lifestyle so that you can accelerate either the rate at which you're paying off debt or the rate at which you are saving? But this type of intensity may not work for everyone, and it's okay to let your daughter know you can have balance in this quest to become a super saver. It will also depend on how badly they want to reach their savings goal.

With some creativity and ingenuity there are many and plenty of ways to save money on life's everyday expenses. Money that is saved can go towards either reducing debt or patting your savings account. Either way you are increasing your net worth and giving yourself a firm financial foundation.

Increasing Your Income to Save More

Increasing your income doesn't always mean adding a side hustle, but that can be a great start. There are other ways to increase your income, including getting a better job, changing careers, asking for a raise, or doing something as simple as adjusting your income tax withholding.

Once you combine increasing your income with decreasing your expenses, you should start to find extra money in your budget that you may not have seen before. That's not money that you should spend without a plan. That's money used for the purposes of meeting your savings goals.

Automating and Systemizing Your Savings

When you find this money, you might find that it's actually difficult to put it away in savings. It doesn't necessarily mean that you are not disciplined but rather that you might not have a great system in place for saving money. One thing you can do to combat this is by setting up a savings workflow.

This sounds fancy, but it's just a way of making sure that your extra money that you work so hard for actually goes into your savings accounts. There are a couple of ways that this can be accomplished.

The good old-fashioned way is simply taking your money in the form of cash and depositing it into your savings account. You can set up a reminder on your calendar phone app that reminds you to withdraw money from your checking account to go into your savings every two weeks.

For your daughter, she may have irregular earnings, so she'll just have to remember to take either a percentage or set amount of her money to put into a savings account.

If you get direct deposits from your job on a regular basis, one of the easiest things you can do is set up an automatic deposit to your savings account. Nowadays, employers will let you set up multiple accounts for your direct deposit.

One thing we do is direct the bulk of my husband's regular paycheck into our checking account and then set aside another larger portion to go into a savings account with an online bank. From there, we divvy up that larger savings deposit into other savings accounts for things like property taxes, house maintenance, and car maintenance.

Another neat savings tactic that's come on the scene is the use of savings apps. There are a number of apps that will either round up purchases or take small amounts from your checking account to help you save money.

I once used an app to save $500 that I used to purchase stock in Nike and Mattel for my youngest daughter. Some of these investing/savings apps will also, in fact, invest your money. They'll use robo-advisory algorithms to invest your money with the best outcome according to your savings goals.

Here are a few options to explore:

- Stash
- Acorns
- Qapital
- Digit
- Tip Yourself

The only thing about investing/savings apps is that you have to really watch the fees. Though they offer an awesome amount of automation so that you don't really have to think about saving, you will pay for it with service fees. Even with the fees, it can be a good way to start a savings habit.

Once you get a little more sophisticated and comfortable managing your money, you can transition to other savings methods that fit you better and are not as expensive.

Retirement Savings

Also, if your employer offers an employer-sponsored retirement savings plan, you should definitely take advantage of that. Though it's not money you can access before you hit official retirement age, it's still a good deal when it comes to saving.

For one, you are contributing money before you pay taxes on it, which represents a huge benefit for you. Many times, your employer will offer a match of 2 percent, 3 percent, or even up to 5 percent of your contributions. This is free money!

There are not many places that you can put your money where you get additional returns on your investment in this way. Also, when you contribute this pre-tax money, your overall tax liability is decreased. The IRS rewards people who save in retirement accounts. So, if your annual income is $48,000 and you contribute at least $4,000, your taxable income ends up being $44,000.[2]

Furthermore, when you save your money in a retirement plan like a 401(k) or 403(b), your money is more likely to grow at a faster pace. Historically, the stock market is known to give returns in the 8 percent to 12 percent range. If your employer can match another 3 percent, that just added to your returns. So this is a savings vehicle that has an element of investing that can really grow your savings in a way that no other can.

---

2   Taylor, Philip, and Elle Martinez. "Can You Deduct 401K Savings From Your Taxes?" The TurboTax Blog, July 23, 2019. https://blog.turbotax.intuit.com /tax-deductions-and-credits-2/can-you -deduct-401k-savings-from-your-taxes -7169/.

CHAPTER 11

Let's Talk Investing

Next to saving, investing is probably one of my next favorite money topics. Investing is like saving but on steroids. I like to talk about investing because it's probably one of the scarier money topics that we face as women.

When people start talking about the stock market, they often assume women don't know much or won't participate in the conversation. If we can start talking about investing with our daughters earlier, they'll be more comfortable talking about investing and will be more likely to become investors themselves.

Again, there's no need to be an expert in order to broach the topic of investing with your daughters. The main thing that you need to know is that investing provides an accelerated way to save your money with the least amount of work. On the flip side of this "super savings" concept, there is risk associated with investing.

Saving your money in a bank account is relatively low-risk. It's also relatively low-return when it comes to reward. Investing your money is higher risk, but the upside has a lot more potential as well.

You might remember that my money story included how my grandmother saved money for my college expenses in a money market account. This is one of the lowest-yielding savings accounts when it comes to earning interest on savings balances.

Though my grandmother was diligent in putting money away for me basically from birth until I turned eighteen, there was barely $2,000 in that account. Why? Because my grandmother didn't understand how to take advantage of compound interest.

You see, she grew up in the era of the Great Depression. The stock market crash of 1929 was burned into the memories of a lot of people and, consequently, gave many folks an aversion to investing in stocks. It was something set aside for the likes of Wall Street tycoons and high-profile money moguls.

I often consider what would have happened if my grandmother would have put that money into a mutual fund or some stock like Walgreens or GE. I'll never know. The cool thing is that I get to rewrite the story for my girls.

Fortunately, I'm alive in a time where I can educate myself and my daughters and we don't have to be afraid of investing. We can be poised to reap the benefits of investing. We can leverage the performance and knowledge and experience of millions of people to say, with certainty, that investing in the stock market is a generally safe, higher-yielding investment that tends to appreciate over time.

Why Invest in the Stock Market Anyway?

If you doubt your knowledge when it comes to investing, I would say the best thing to do is understand the outcomes. Once you see the potential for your investments to grow, you'll start to find extra money to invest where you couldn't before.

For example, $1,000 invested in each of these companies around 1985 would have yielded the following amounts today (June 11, 2019):

- Apple (APPL)—$3,152,837
- Walgreens (WBA)—$722,769
- Nike (NKE)—$3,624,628[1]

---

1   Backtest Portfolio Asset Allocation. Accessed November 12, 2019. https://www
.portfoliovisualizer.com/backtest-portfolio.

Can you believe these numbers? It should make you want to find $1,000 to invest in a company as soon as you possibly can.

It's important to note that even though this $1,000 initial investment in each of the three companies grew to epic proportions, there were also times where these companies lost quite a bit of value.

This is what's scary for most people. To put $20,000 into an investment and see the value drop by a third or even in half can be unsettling. But over a 30-year period (even with dips), the value of stock prices usually recover in a way that most people find it hard to believe.

The point here is to know that the value of stocks can go up and down. But if you stay in, the value (and the price) generally goes up so that you can benefit from the profits. Imagine buying $1,000 of stock and being able to sell it for $2 million or $3 million in 20 or 30 years! In order to get this kind of return, you've actually got to start investing and stay in it for the long haul.

Another concept you should be familiar with is compound interest. One of my favorite tools to demonstrate how money can grow is the compound interest calculator at the Investor.gov website.

With this tool, you can simulate different scenarios to see the outcomes of investing a specific amount of money for a specific amount of time. For example, if you can use the calculator to figure out how much $50 invested per month yields over 20 years at about a 5 percent return rate, you'll see that the results are still pretty mind-boggling, generating close to $20,000.

In this scenario, you only contributed around $12,000 but you got almost $20,000 out of the deal! How? Compound interest!

Compound interest is what happens when your investments appreciate, then you reinvest the profits for even more profits. You get to eat, sleep, play, work, and love your life while your investments are growing, appreciating, and multiplying.

If you ever heard the saying, "Your money should work for you and not the other way around," this is exactly what people mean. When you set aside money to invest, it's like having another employee bringing in a paycheck on your behalf. It's no wonder that Albert Einstein said that compound interest is the eighth wonder of the world!

Again, I don't think most people get to see these simulations up-close-and-personal, so they don't really fathom the power of compound interest. I know that I didn't understand it for a long time either. But once you do get it, it will change the way you'll want to earn money forever.

Most folks don't even understand that if you've got enough money in investments, that money will create regular income for you. For example, in a decent market, a $1 million portfolio could earn $50,000 per year.

If you can live off this amount of money each year, your investments could sustain your lifestyle. The best part? You don't ever touch the principal! So then, the next year, you'll still have $1 million that will make another $50,000 for you. If you can't live off $50,000 per year, then double your balance to $2 million, where you can earn $100,000 per year.

I know it sounds weird to say, just make $1 million and your life will be easy and your investments will sustain you, but it's not impossible. It will take some diligence and creativity, but it can certainly be done.

Now that you know about the awesome potential outcomes of investing, you should be motivated to learn more about investing. But I know it can feel scary. I'll admit that once we paid off debt, I started saving money like crazy. But I was afraid to invest my money.

However, once I plugged into a community of financial bloggers, it became apparent that investing would have to be the next money milestone for us to tackle. So what did I do?

I took time to read books about investing. Some of them were terribly complicated and confusing. I did not take that as a sign that I should just forget about it—I simply realized that not everyone's method of teaching and communicating about investing concepts was for me.

After a little more searching, I found people who were more like me. They were young professionals close to my age and had had similar life experiences. Some of them may have grown up poor or had some traumatic events take place as pertains to money, like massive student loan debt or getting caught up in the 2008 housing bubble.

It wasn't that these people were more knowledgeable than any others I had encountered on my quest to learn about investing. I just felt like they spoke a language that was more on my wavelength. They had books, courses, and a plethora of information on how regular everyday people could become investors.

One particular resource was an eCourse by Mabel Nunez, the CEO and founder of Girls on the Money. I felt like the material she presented was basic yet informative enough for both myself *and* my daughters to learn about investing. Yep, I made my girls take her course right along with me.

It took us the entire summer to get through the course. I made sure that I set aside time so that we could watch the videos and discuss them. That summer was a great one because we took that investing course and learned how to pick and invest in individual stocks.

I felt it was really important for us to learn about investing because of our family's circumstances. Because both of my daughters earn money regularly as paid entertainers, I want them to put their money away so it can take that 20 or 30 years to become massive fortunes. As their mom, I wanted to learn how to do this for them, then make sure they understood how to do it on their own, too.

By the time they reached seven and eleven years old, they were logging into their brokerage and purchasing shares of the stocks they have been researching. I'm so thankful that I've taught my daughters to buy stocks as if they were a pair of jeans from Old Navy. I believe we can all lead our daughters into this kind of behavior.

Now, I want to be real about the experience of learning about stocks and investing with my daughters. There was whining and lots of it. Many times, I would turn on the videos and my kids would straight zone out on me.

They forgot lots of things, too. I would pause the video, try to break things down into their language, and sometimes they would forget or pretend not to understand. At times, it was pretty frustrating.

When you're having these money conversations with your daughters, it can be challenging, but we have to remember our job as "farmers" to plant those seeds. Even if my daughters can't consciously recall a lot of the concepts that were taught in the eCourse we took, I'm happy that we went through the experience for the sake of planting seeds.

But one thing I'd like to emphasize specifically regarding investing is that even if the concepts you learn are fleeting, what remains true is your growing balance! To this day, my daughters have tangible evidence of taking that course and learning to buy stocks.

Those stocks they purchased are still in their brokerage accounts and growing in value. If they are able to stay with their holdings for 10, 20, or 30 years, I can only imagine the amount of appreciation they'll muster.

I tell you this story for a couple of reasons. The first reason is that learning to invest doesn't have to be hard and it doesn't have to be complicated. If you pick up resources that are too difficult for you to digest, just keep looking for a resource from which you can actually learn.

How to Get Started as a Newbie Investor

Before we dive into how to get started, I should clarify that if you invest in your 401(k), or if you have real estate, a small business, or you just have a few dollars in a few simple stocks, you should consider yourself an investor. That's all it takes.

Let's say you have done none of these things. You haven't put money away in a 401(k) or any other type of retirement account. You don't own any real estate and you've never purchased any stocks.

Unfortunately, you haven't yet started your small business. Despite this, you can still become an investor relatively easily.

As mentioned in the savings section, the lowest hanging fruit to start with would be investing in your employer's retirement plan. That could be a 401(k) or 403(b) or even some flavor of an IRA.

According to the U.S. Census and the National Institute on Retirement Security, 57 percent of US workers have $0 in employer sponsored retirement plans.[2] This means there are millions of people who have the option to become investors, usually in a tax-deferred manner, that simply don't.

As we saw in a previous chapter, even when people do invest or amass assets, women end up having less money and assets than their male counterparts. The great news is that we can teach our daughters and other young women in our lives to become investors through employer-sponsored retirement savings plans.

Because you contribute from your paycheck, oftentimes with pre-tax money, it's probably one of the best things you can do to become an investor. It's not an investing option any of us should ignore!

Once you cover that base, you also have additional investing options. You can open a brokerage account with a discount broker like TD Ameritrade, E-Trade, or Vanguard. These accounts are free to open and simply charge a fee for every trade you execute (that is, buying and selling).

Once you open your account, you can simply transfer money from your bank account to your brokerage account so that it is funded and ready to purchase investments like stocks, bonds, mutual funds, or ETFs (exchange traded funds).

Now because this is not a book that is solely about investing, I'm just going to drop some terms here and you'll have to do the work to find out what some of these things mean and get knowledgeable

---

2   O'Connell, Brian. "U.S. Census Date Reveals $0 Median Retirement Savings Balance." AdvisorNews, October 2, 2018. https://advisornews.com/innarticle/u-s-census-date-reveals-0-median-retirement-savings-balance.

on your own. If there's something you don't understand or are not familiar with, take notes to look them up later and understand them as investing concepts.

I think this is a great activity that you can do with your daughter. If you don't know what an exchange-traded fund is and why it might be a better alternative to mutual funds, both mom and daughter can learn together.

After all, there's nothing more powerful than showing her, first-hand, that it's okay to pursue something that you don't fully understand, sometimes with fear in your heart and doubt in your mind.

Lastly, one of the most wonderful developments of the last 10 to 15 years are fintech apps that help you do everything from manage your budget, to automate your savings, to even invest in the stock market.

These apps are pretty effective with the younger generation. Our tech-savvy young ones are visual and like the immediacy of the Internet. Combined with data crunched in real time and packed into easy-to-read and easy-to-understand charts, investing apps help even the most hesitant novice get started on their investing journey.

With a few taps, these apps can show you historical data, ratios, and related news topics so that you can make an informed decision on investment purchases without a lot of work. Apps can be a great way to break into investing for the novice investor.

With that being said, also note that investing apps are great as a learning tool but sometimes, the fees associated with them can be a bit much in comparison to some of your returns. If you're working on learning to invest and teaching the same to your daughter, these apps are a good place to start, but eventually you want to move to more economical platforms (like the discount brokers mentioned above).

Here are some of my favorite ways to become an investor using a smartphone:

- Stash
- Acorns

- Robinhood
- Worthy Bonds

Another great way to invest in stocks, especially for kids, is a platform called Stockpile. The nice thing about Stockpile is that you can purchase fractional shares of stocks.

Say, for example, one of your favorite stocks is trading at $100 or more a share. With Stockpile, you can purchase small amounts in increments of $1, $5, $10, or more. They are also available as gift cards. Many of your local grocery stores carry fractional stock shares in the form of Stockpile gift cards. Once purchased, they can be redeemed and tracked in a free Stockpile account. It's another good way for kids to get familiar with investing.

I'm Still Overwhelmed with Investing

If you still feel like there's no way that you can understand investing enough to either learn alongside of your daughters or teach them what you know, that's okay. The goal is to reduce the feeling of being overwhelmed and get you to the place where you feel comfortable enough to actually start investing.

If you feel like investing is too complicated and gives you a headache just thinking about it, just focus on getting started. If you need to engage help along the way, then you should feel okay with doing that as well. Not everyone has to be a DIY investor.

Fortunately, with the advent of robo-advisors and fee-only financial planners, you have several options when it comes to finding someone that can help you start your investing journey.

If you don't have millions of dollars in assets, you can engage a fee-only financial planner who will charge a flat rate or hourly fee to help you come up with a financial game plan that works for your specific goals and needs in life.

Should you pay a fee? In some cases, it makes sense. If you know you need the help but can't work with a traditional financial planner because you don't have enough assets, fee-only planners could work for you. There are other financial advisors who are paid commissions by selling you certain types of financial products—whether you need them or not.

If it's possible, I would discourage you from going this route because sometimes these "professionals" may not direct you toward products that are in your best interest. When looking for someone to help you out, make sure they are fiduciary, which means that they are committed to acting in your best interest no matter how much of a commission they might make by recommending another financial product.

It's okay to need help, but it's not okay to procrastinate. Whatever you have to do, get it done so you can start taking advantage of the time value of money. Your daughters are watching, and they need someone to model on this investing journey!

CHAPTER 12

Making Money Now (or Later)

We live in a time when it's easier to make money than ever. You can take to the Internet and become a star no matter how old you are or where you come from. Furthermore, the World Wide Web has leveled the playing field and makes it easy for almost anyone to become a brand, influencer, retailer, or service provider.

It used to be that you would talk to your kids about making money in a place in time that seemed far, far away. But with kids being able to earn money earlier and earlier in their lives, it means you have to talk about the dynamics of your little ones earning money as minors.

Can kids really earn money right now? You betcha.

With just a few clicks, kids can start dog-walking businesses or lemonade stands or start selling trinkets to friends and families. Back in the day, these ventures would be small-time enterprises that might just take up a few hours of your kids' day.

However, the Internet multiplies efforts and makes it much easier to actually start a real business whether you are a kid or not. There are apps, Facebook groups, mass email service providers, and plenty of other ways for the word to spread online about pretty much any business your child can start these days.

Perhaps the biggest question around working or pursuing a business venture will be whether or not to let your child spend their time earning money or focusing on their education. I know that many parents tell their kids, "Relax, making money is not the focus of your life right now. Getting your education is the focus of your life."

For a long time, that was true. It's exactly why child labor laws were put into place. In the early years of our country, many kids had to skip out on their education in order to work for the family. As a result, much of the population was undereducated and largely remained illiterate. This caused many people to earn wages that just covered basic living needs.

The founding fathers of this nation envisioned a free public education system to help combat the ills of a poorly educated population. They wanted the American people to be educated enough to make good decisions about legislation and elected officials while becoming productive members of society.

How else could people vote and decide on important policies that would impact their life unless they had critical thinking skills and knowledge to make informed decisions? Education was the key.

Fast forward a few hundred years, and the world looks a lot different now. For one, knowledge, information, and instruction is so much easier to obtain and is getting less expensive by the minute. If you really need to do anything, including some highly specialized occupations, you can consult the World Wide Web. Ever heard of YouTube University? It's how thousands of experts are being created each day on just about any topic you can think of.

The point I'm making is that though education is really important, the way that people are becoming educated is changing. Yes, you should be well-versed on reading, writing, and arithmetic. You should be able to do basic math computation and communicate well in both verbal and written manners. Those are immensely important skills.

But at the end of the day, you might have to decide whether or not you can create an environment where your child can thrive in school while also making money. There may come a point where your child can do both. And there may come a point where you'll have to choose one.

Imagine your child starting a company that earns five or six figures a year. Do you let them focus on their company or do you make them focus on school? Could you create an environment where they are able to do both? For example, more people are taking advantage of homeschooling because it can provide that type of opportunity.

Our family started homeschooling because we felt like it was a good choice for kids based on the neighborhood in which we lived. But we continued to homeschool because it also helped us support our kids' careers in acting and entertainment. Not only that, we've been able to support our kids as they learn about the world through travel, extensive STEM studies, and courses on entrepreneurship.

Yes, homeschooling can be more work, but it also creates an environment where your child can learn while also exploring different ways to earn money. In other words, your kids can become proficient in important life undertakings, like entrepreneurship, right now.

To some, it might sound far-fetched to think that your child could be so successful in a business or earning money that you'll have to figure out a way to get their schooling done. But believe me, there's a future ahead wherein kids will start earning more money earlier and earlier in their lives and will do so with greater potential.

Sure, your kid can offer babysitting services to people on the block, but just imagine what can happen when they create a profile on a babysitting app. They can become pretty busy. At some point you'll have to make a determination of whether or not it's a good idea for them to work more or focus on their schooling more or have some balance of both.

The best thing you can do is come up with parameters right now. Because when the pressure is on and your daughter is in front of you whining about all the things she needs and all the things she wants, it will be hard to resist the urge to give in to her request.

At the end of the day, you might find that your daughter really wants to focus on making money. Being a teenager is expensive; all the things that they need to buy might mean that she'll have to work more and more. So, you'll need to have a plan in place concerning what that might look like.

For example, you might have set requirements such as maintaining a regular bedtime, keeping a certain grade point average, or even forcing your daughter to create a budget. This is also a good opportunity to teach your daughter about trading dollars for hours.

Your daughter might think it's absolutely essential to have that brand-new, designer purse. But when you show her how many hours it takes from her life to acquire "things," this might bring a perspective to the conversation that helps her understand that there are better ways to spend her time. She might even find more efficient ways of acquiring the things she wants (i.e. let income-producing assets cover her expenses, shop at the thrift store, etc.).

Even if your child doesn't start a huge business, she may want to make more money with chores. She may complain that her allowance isn't enough. That's still a conversation you'll have to have when your daughter insists that she needs more money or wants for things.

In fact, here are some responses you should be prepared to address when you talk to your daughter about making money.

I Need More Money

It seems like no matter how much money your daughter makes, it's never going to be enough. If she is a teenager, she is probably very much into her image and her social life. She may want to keep up with her peers, the latest fashion trends, and participate in all the fun activities. This is going to cost money—potentially lots of it.

This is a great time to discuss how your daughter could reduce some of her wants—i.e., she'll have to prioritize the most important needs based on her available resources. The other option is to find ways to meet her needs in a more economical way. This will mean taking the initiative to find deals and being creative and inventive to avoid spending a lot of money.

One thing I recently did with my daughter when this issue came up was that I asked her to make a monthly budget of all her expenses. Though I did not promise that she would get more money, I asked her to complete this activity so she could see on paper what it took to meet her needs and wants money-wise.

Once she outlined her needs, we were able to discuss a plan of action regarding how she could either reduce some of her expenses, postpone them for a time when she could make more money, or be granted more opportunities to do chores that would help her make money.

If you do it this way, you are trying to help your daughter see that more money isn't always the solution. Sometimes, it's a matter of managing what you already have access to in a better way.

You don't have to be like me and get annoyed at the "I need more money" conversation. I've learned that this is a great opportunity to discuss the idea that more money may not help but better financial management can.

I Want This Shiny New Thing

Inevitably, your daughter will want new shiny things. She may even have the money for it or a perfectly hatched plan to get it. The only problem is it might be so exorbitant or unnecessary that it really wouldn't even make sense to have a serious conversation around it.

Before you write the conversation off, just remember that no money conversation should be off limits. If your 17-year-old daughter wants to take the $40,000 you saved for her college fund and purchase a brand-new Benz, you might be tempted to shut the conversation down right away. You might think there's no sense in even entertaining the conversation.

Even if you feel like your daughter is not a totally rational being at the moment, you still need to treat her as if she were. You'd be surprised at how she will rise to the occasion.

The first thing you want to get down to is why she feels like she needs to have a fancy car like a Benz at age 16 or 17. Once you get to the bottom of that, you might also ask her about the kind of return she'll see on that "investment." Putting $40,000 into a depreciating asset is not the best idea, especially when she has her whole life in front of her.

Ask her about her dreams and goals. Ask her if she believes that those things will take money. (By the way, this line of questioning works for pretty much any ridiculous money conversation you think you'll have to have with your daughter when it comes to making big money decisions.)

When you explain to her that the money she spends should be used to add value to her life and not take away from it, you can also let her know that buying a car that loses value will not accomplish that goal. The idea here is to put her money where it can grow in value.

Things that increase in value are often intangibles and may include a college education, real estate, or even a business opportunity. Though none of these types of investments are guaranteed to yield a return (in fact, they could also lose value; that's why they are investments, because they have a level of risk associated with them), experience tells us that using money to acquire any one of these types of assets will far outweigh buying a depreciating asset like a car.

Again, don't expect your teenager to act like she's been hit on the head and through some magical type of beneficial head injury, she has come to her senses and changed her desires overnight. These are conversations you will likely have to have over and over again. You'll plant the seed, then you'll water it and keep watering it until it grows and it looks like your daughter will finally make sensible decisions when it comes to money.

It's My Money

If your daughter is already making money because she's an industrious go-getter, it will be hard to explain to her why she can't do whatever she wants with her money. If she's been babysitting since she was 11 years old and managed to save $5,000 by the time she's 16 that's a great accomplishment.

But what if she wants to use that money in a way that is totally counter to what you have taught her over the years about money? Maybe she wants to buy her boyfriend some DJ equipment or get a really elaborate tattoo. Whatever it is, you have to be prepared to have this conversation about why your daughter can't really spend *her* money any way that she wants.

For one, you are her parent and while she is under your care you get to make decisions on her behalf that you feel are in her best interest. In fact, in most states, parents are legally bound to operate in the best interest of their child. That means making money decisions for them, even if they have their own financial account.

The fact is, your daughter can only make and save up money because you provide an environment that allows her to do so. She can make money as a dog walker because you drop her off to various homes in the neighborhood. She can make money as a babysitter because you provide a home for her in which to babysit. She can make money selling gadgets and widgets because you may have given her startup money. You also provide a place for her to live and food for her to eat so she can use her money for her business needs.

I have this very situation with my girls. Yes, they have money saved up from some of their acting gigs (and believe me, they want to access it every other day). But the truth of the matter is that they would not be gainfully employed in the industry if I had not taken time to get them to auditions, pay for new headshots, invest in acting classes, get workers permits, and the list goes on.

The long and short of it is that you enable your daughters to earn money and save it, so you do have a say in how it's spent. Nevertheless, it's very possible that this conversation could go awry because kids are kids and they may not understand this reasoning. Just remember, this is one of those things you'll mention over and over again when your daughter is begging you to drop $2,000 on tickets to Coachella.

This conversation should also always involve the idea that your daughter should be saving a percentage of her earnings. Since you do have the final say in what happens to her money while she's a minor, make sure putting away money in a savings account or investment account is part of the conversation.

We are living in different times now and it's true that many kids will have the opportunity to earn money in many different ways. Regardless of what their professional pursuits entail, you'll want to set guidelines and rules so that it's clear what you expect and what your daughter should expect in this situation.

Hopefully, you will have already created a game plan, so you'll be equipped and prepared to confidently enter a conversation with your daughter about her money as a minor living in your home. Yes, you'll have your own requirements and ways of doing things, but you should also be flexible and open to negotiating and humoring ideas that your daughters will have about making money as a minor. Ultimately, you are the parent and she is the child, but I believe it's possible for you to work together as a team through civil conversation to come up with a great solution when it comes to working, schooling, earning money, and striking a balance between it all.

CHAPTER 13

Let's Talk College

I talked a little bit about college and how that might pan out for my girls in previous chapters, but I believe that this topic deserves its very own chapter.

College is such a huge financial commitment and can have an even bigger impact on the way your life turns out, and thus this is a conversation that should be had early on. Depending on your child's disposition towards college, you might need to talk about it frequently.

The decisions you make about college can change the course of your life forever—from taking out loans to choosing a major and even deciding to study abroad, college activities and choices can affect the quality of your life.

It's estimated that Americans now owe $1.5 trillion in student loan debt.[1] Almost 12 percent of student loans are in default.[2] Supposedly, the student loan bubble will be the next to pop and have a domino effect that could cause a recession-like effect on the US economy.

---

1 Berman, Jillian. "Here's Why America's $1.5 Trillion Student-Loan Crisis Has Spiralled out of Control." MarketWatch, July 6, 2019. https://www.market watch.com/story/why-financial-education-wont-solve-the-15-trillion -student-loan-crisis-2019-06-27.
2 "U.S. Student Loan Debt Statistics for 2019." Student Loan Hero, February 4, 2019. https://studentloanhero.com/student-loan-debt-statistics/.

I'm not trying to sound like a conspiracy theorist, but the proof is in the numbers. Almost 50 percent of the United States's assets are held in student loan debt.[3] There are politicians trying to figure out ways to relieve the pressure of individual borrowers while ensuring that the government retains these loan assets for its own survival.

Sure, it might sound like a fantastic plan to forgive most of the student loan debt, but there are real roadblocks to this becoming a reality. For one, some studies show that a lot of this debt is held by high earners.[4] People who are now in the medical profession or are practicing as lawyers may have a large amount of debt, but they also may have relatively higher income.

In order to forgive the debt, the income that was expected to come in to the government with the repayment plans will have to be replaced in some way. What do you think the primary way will be? Because the government does not produce or create anything, the only way they can raise revenue is through raising taxes.

How would you feel about paying more taxes to cover the student loans for your urologist or neighbor who is a corporate tax lawyer and a high six-figure earner? You may not have many qualms about this, but I can tell you that politically it's just a difficult problem to tackle.

The point in all of this is not to get political or to speculate on how public policy could affect student loans. However, the best position is just to assume that things will be as they always were. If you take out student loans to cover the cost of your education you will, more than likely, be responsible for paying them back.

---

3 Mislinski, Jill. "The Fed's Financial Accounts: What Is Uncle Sam's Largest Asset?" advisorperspectives.com, September 9, 2019. https://www.advisor perspectives.com/dshort/commentaries/2019/09/24/the-fed-s-financial -accounts-what-is-uncle-sam-s-largest-asset.

4 Chubb, Chad. "High-Earning Millennials Have a Surprising Student Debt Problem." www.kiplinger.com. Kiplingers Personal Finance, May 29, 2019. https://www.kiplinger.com/article/college/T025-C032-S014-high-earning -millennials-student-debt-problem.html.

My College Drama

The discussion now becomes how do you determine if 1) college is worth it for you and 2) the career that you choose will actually justify the amount of money that you take out for college.

I do wish someone would have had this conversation with me before I took out almost $30,000 in student loans to get a liberal arts degree.

To be clear, I don't want to paint the picture that my college education was not worth the money I spent on it. It was indeed worth every penny. As someone who enjoyed academia overall, college was an extremely intellectually stimulating place for me and I remember it with fondness. I do believe that it prepared me for the life that I'm now living as a personal finance and small business writer and advocate for financial literacy.

However, I do wish someone sat down with me and showed me what it meant to have a $30,000 student loan balance with a private company. I never even thought about how I'd be affected if I didn't have flexible payment options like federal student loans have. Without programs like forbearance, deferment, income-based repayment, and other federal student loan payment remediation options, I was stuck simply paying the bill as it came to me every month.

Furthermore, I never even thought twice about having to pay the money back. On top of that, I was delusional about my income prospects. I was such a great test taker and had a fairly decent GPA (for a chronic absentee and dedicated party girl), I just knew that there were some six-figure jobs waiting for me after college.

I was in for a rude awakening when I found out that my general Spanish/Economics degree did not afford me many lucrative job options. Despite having multiple internships in telecommunications and business administration, it seems like I could only find jobs in that area that paid $30,000 or less a year.

Technically, there was the possibility to get a job that could pay me sixty or seventy thousand or more per year. My mom was a nurse and had spent the last few years of my college career working for a number of pharmaceutical companies. She suggested that I apply to be a pharmaceutical sales representative because they would pay a salary more in line with what I had fantasized about while I was working hard for my degree.

After taking her advice, applying for some companies, I did actually have a pretty sweet pharmaceutical sales representative job lined up for me right before graduation. It looks like that $30,000 loan wasn't such a terrible idea after all. College wasn't a waste of time and despite having a very general liberal arts degree I could still earn something close to six figures. In my mind, I thought it would be just a matter of a few years before I actually hit six figures. I was a genius!

Then real life happened to me. The company that had made that dream offer reneged. They found out that I had some problems with my driver's license that would prevent me from driving for at least another year. I couldn't be a sales rep if I was unable to drive. My dream job vanished and I panicked.

To make matters worse, September 11th happened. And of course, I would never minimize the fateful day that changed the course of our nation's history forever, but I think that many people will agree with me about what was happening at the time. Not only did that terrorist attack scare everyone to their core, but it had a huge negative impact on the entire US economy.

If you were graduating from college at that time, you know how difficult it was to get a job. In fact, some people who were already employed were laid off because a recession started.

Though I was really disappointed about losing the pharmaceutical sales job, I was eventually able to find an inside sales job. I would be an account representative that provided computer and related technology equipment to government entities like schools, hospitals, and park districts. The base salary was pretty low, but there was tons of opportunity to make commission. Too bad I was a lousy salesperson.

I'm not going to go into all the factors that made that job a nightmare for me, but suffice to say that I didn't stay long and I never really made that much money. But guess what still came in? The monthly statements for my student loan never let me down.

This was such a trying time for me. I thought I had done everything everyone told me to do. I did well in school. I went to college. I even took out loans to "invest" in myself to complete my degree. I thought that I was supposed to make enough money to pay back the loans and enjoy gainful employment for the rest of my life.

I also discovered that corporate America was hard. I didn't like the politics, bureaucracy, and the uncertainty of the nine-to-five life. I felt like I could contribute so much in terms of my innovation and creativity but much of that went untapped because there was a larger corporate agenda. As a result, I just never succeeded in corporate America.

But your student loans don't care about your need to be creative. They just care about being paid back. The sooner you can have this kind of conversation with your daughter the better.

If you've got a nightmare college/student loan story, make sure you share that really early. Talk about what you wish you would have done differently and what you made in the process. You should also talk about your daughter's plans and ideas when it comes to college.

Figuring Out If You Can Afford College

There are so many variables to this conversation. A degree in higher education has so many tangible and intangible benefits that it becomes difficult to measure whether or not the return-on-investment is in line with your daughter's expectations for her life.

Hopefully, you talked about hopes and dreams and your daughter has already painted a picture of her ideal life. It may include some highly specialized profession in STEM or some otherwise very specific career path like dentistry. We all know that these careers will definitely require a college degree.

But we also know that even higher earners can get caught in a cycle of paycheck-to-paycheck living despite their relatively high income.[5] Whether your daughter wants to be a photographer or a pediatrician, it's best to do the research to find out how much her career choice will yield over her lifetime.

You can go to the U.S. Bureau of Labor Statistics website and check out the Occupational Handbook Outlook, where you can research and get salary estimates for various occupations. There are other websites that you can go on to get an idea of what your daughter could earn over her lifetime in a certain career or profession, too.

Keep in mind that your daughter may or may not be ready to declare her life's purpose just yet. That's okay. You might be able to get a few options from her to explore some suitable careers and related salaries. You just want to start the flow of ideas so you can find related salary figures. It's time to start doing some basic math to figure out if investing in a college degree is worth the potential cost.

From here, look at some potential college options and tuition costs. To keep things simple, don't factor in scholarships or financial aid into the equation. We're just looking at the raw cost of attending college for four years with a major related to the type of career your daughter wants.

Once you figure out tuition figures then it's okay to calculate how much four years of college could cost. Then, let your daughter take a look at the income prospects.

This exercise is pretty unsophisticated because, again, we won't be factoring in financial aid, which could greatly decrease the cost of college, and we will not be factoring in things like raises, increases in college tuition from now to the time your daughter reaches age 18, or cost-of-living adjustments that tend to happen over a person's career.

---

5   Adcock, Steve. "Why People Who Earn a Lot of Money Still Can't Pay the Bills." MarketWatch, December 23, 2018. https://www.marketwatch.com/story/why -people-who-earn-a-lot-of-money-still-cant-pay-the-bills-2018-12-20.

In other words, if she starts in a profession making $30,000 a year, it's very possible that toward the end of her perhaps 30-year working career she could have triple or quadruple that figure.

Now the clincher might be that looking at a $100,000 tuition bill may seem like nothing when someone could make $30,000 or more a year for 20 to 30 years. If you do the math someone could potentially earn $600,000 to almost a million dollars over their lifetime. So it would seem like a no-brainer to drop the hundred thousand in tuition and proceed to collect your million dollars. Seems like a great return, right?

Well, this could certainly be the case in a perfect world. But let's talk about some things that could drastically change the outcome of your daughter's earning potential and return on investment for her college tuition expenses.

We already mentioned that women have a unique set of circumstances that could potentially reduce their earning potential over their lifetime. Women can be unemployed or underemployed when they have children, or even other members of their family, to take care of.

Women can be underemployed in general, meaning they are overqualified for a position and are earning less because their employment is not on par with their skills, training, and experience. We also discussed the gender wage gap, where women earn 79 cents on the dollar compared to men.[6]

It's also worth noting that earnings don't equal wealth accumulation. Though someone could earn almost $1,000,000 over their lifetime as an employee, we are witnessing that the people who should have accumulated the most wealth, the baby boomer generation,

---

6 Elkins, Kathleen. "Here's How Much Men and Women Earn at Every Age." CNBC. CNBC, April 2, 2019. https://www.cnbc.com/2019/04/02/heres-how -much-men-and-women-earn-at-every-age.html.

actually have very little in savings and very little to show for earning that cool million over their lifetime.

As you paint the picture of how student loans can impact savings potential and overall quality of life. If estimated payments of $300 to $500 a month would put a damper on that, then talk about how your daughter can minimize the impact of student loans on her life by either choosing a higher-earning career or looking for scholarships and grants that could reduce this number. College can be a very worthwhile investment, but it's best to get the numbers to make sense as much as possible so the bill doesn't haunt your daughter for decades to come.

The Numbers Don't Work; Now What?

More than likely after you've gone through this long drawn-out exercise, your daughter may feel a little discouraged. She may have found out that the career she wants to go into really doesn't pay as much as she thought compared to the amount of student loans she'd have to take out to pursue it.

Maybe the student loan payment per month is just a little too much to swallow provided your daughter wants to travel after college or take time to pursue a profession that is lower-paying to start off.

If this is the case, there's no need to be discouraged. Nowadays, there are so many options when it comes to education that if you do some planning, you should be able to find a solution that works for your daughter's pocketbook, desired career path, and preferred quality of life.

Firstly, if it doesn't look like throwing tens of thousands of dollars into a degree is a good investment based on the income prospects, then there are plenty of variables that you can tweak to make your daughter's college dream come to pass.

Perhaps the first course of action would be to find out if an actual degree is needed for your daughter's preferred career. Would it be possible for her to enter into that profession with either a certificate, apprenticeship, internship, or some other form of experience that doesn't have to be a college degree? If it's possible, you might explore the possibility of going one of these routes which can be much less expensive than an entire four-year degree.

Next, ask your daughter if she could do something related to her profession that may not require a full degree. Now, you don't want to be in the business of discouraging or downgrading your daughter's dream.

In this case, you'll have to tread very lightly and know your child. If she is claiming that she wants to be a pediatrician and will stay in school for the 10 or 15 years it takes to become a doctor, then you should definitely encourage her in that direction.

But if your experience tells you that this may not be the case, you could ask your daughter about other related careers such as nursing, pharmacology, dentistry, veterinary medicine, becoming an ultrasound technician, etc. This could give her the chance to explore fields related to medicine and decide later on if she wants to go all the way by becoming an MD.

Let's assume that career path and getting a degree are nonnegotiables. The career path that your daughter has chosen is what she wants and her mind is made up. However, the large student loan bill could still put a damper on her college plans.

Here's where you'll have to be creative and work as a team. First up, your options could include revising your choice of colleges. She could choose to go to a state college to get in-state tuition, which is often cheaper than going to a private college.

Another option could be to take classes like general education courses at a community college. Those credit hours tend to be much less expensive than credit hours at a four-year university. Many people have successfully completed their college career by starting at a community college. In fact, my brother did a three-year stint at a local community college and is now a proud PhD in civil engineering.

The next step would be to consider different types of financial aid options. You can include work study loans and even institution-specific scholarships if you are eligible for these options. If you don't anticipate that financial aid will be enough to cover college tuition, the next option would be to try scholarships to make up the difference.

The key with scholarships is that you have to start early. And by early, I mean your daughter should begin thinking about her academic career by the time she reaches junior high. Those grades will determine how she's placed in high school, and of course beginning with her freshman year of high school, she'll want to be sure that her GPA, extracurricular activities, and test scores increase her eligibility for scholarship options.

Finally, if you're reading this and your daughter is still pretty young, the good news is that you actually have time to start saving for college. Studies show that kids are six times more likely to attend college if they have a savings account in their name.[7]

Whether or not your child wants to actually go to college doesn't make a difference. The fact that you're saving money sends a huge message and it will be nice for her to have the money to spend on other things should she decide that college isn't the direction she wants to take.

If you start saving up the money, at least she'll have it along with the flexibility to make the decision about college. As we saw in the investing chapter, you can save as little as $50 a year over 20 years to get to a $20,000 balance. Sure, your daughter will need more than that for college, but just get started. You can get to $200 and $300 payments later on if you have to.

This approach works best if you are able to start earlier than later. Even if you feel like it's too late to start saving, every little bit helps.

---

7 Martin, Jessica. "Kids with Savings Accounts in Their Name Six Times More Likely to Attend College." The Source: Washington University in St. Louis, January 13, 2016. https://source.wustl.edu/2011/04/kids-with-savings-accounts-in-their-name-six-times-more-likely-to-attend-college/.

Start when you can with what you have and show your daughter that you are confident in her dreams.

Right now, I've got a daughter who is just wrapping up her freshman year as a homeschool student. She's fully expecting to enter high school as a sophomore in a few months. Almost every day we have a conversation about her grades and being diligent with building up her professional and academic profile if college is on her list of things to do.

I'm watching her to gauge how her actions line up with her stated desire to go to college. Fortunately, we've been able to save quite a bit of money up for her. I've been clear to her that this money can be used for college education or for her first real estate purchase.

I keep planting those conversational seeds with her so that she understands she has an option and that she also has resources. As a result, she's been pretty diligent with her schoolwork and seems like she's doing whatever it takes to either go to college or have access to the funds to help her start life when she leaves my home.

I realize that we have somewhat of a unique situation. With my kids earning money in acting and entertainment and having their own savings accounts to help cover college or the cost of starting life in general, it seems like my daughters will have a great chance at starting off life without debt. In fact, they may even have a head start depending on what they decide to do.

Everyone isn't in this situation, so I want to keep talking about options that can help people who are on different sides of the college readiness spectrum. So far, I think we've covered a lot of scenarios that many people can benefit from. But there's one that probably a lot of people will find themselves in.

Now, let's say that it's the eleventh hour—maybe it's July—and your daughter is slated to start college in the coming months. Unfortunately, you have no money for her. There's nothing saved up to cover her tuition, room/board, books, or expenses.

Hopefully, you've at least let your daughter know that there isn't any money or that you won't be able to help her as much as you thought you could. Please take my advice and don't wait until the last minute to have this conversation!

My heart breaks every time my husband tells me about returning to college for his sophomore year and finding out that his parents were not able to help him with tuition. He showed up ready to move into the dorms for a second year and ended up having to go home that very day. That was a really trying time for him.

You don't have to go through that, and you don't have to put your daughter through that. If you feel like this could be the case, make sure you talk to her well before she's ready to leave. If you can, even start to have this talk around freshman year (because by then you'll know how much you have saved and have a good idea of what you're able to contribute).

Finally, other options include taking a gap year or forgoing college altogether. These options are not to be taken lightly, but you can weigh the pros and cons based on your daughter's needs, personality, and career choice.

The good news is that taking time off from school doesn't mean that your child won't be successful in life. In fact, my oldest child wavers between going to college and not going to college, and I'm actually okay with that.

Is College Right for Every Child?

The fact of the matter is that someone who decides to start a business in high school versus someone who decides to go to college for an undergraduate or graduate degree actually has a real chance of making a decent living for themselves. In some cases, we find that some people can forgo college and do even better professionally. For example, Apple CEO Tim Cook confessed that over half of Apple's US employment in 2018 was made up of people who did not have four-year degrees. Though we don't know much about the earnings or quality of life of these non-degreed employees, we can see that it's definitely possible to attain gainful employment along with success in life without a college degree. This can be especially true if you are able to reduce lifestyle costs and put more money into savings and investments despite earning less than college-educated counterparts.

Am I suggesting that you let your eight-year-old quit school in order to focus on her dog-walking business? Of course not, that would be ridiculous.

But when it comes to having the conversation around making money in pursuing education, I think it's a matter of being flexible and understanding your child. For example, my oldest child doesn't really care much for the academic rigor or structure of school. She's told me on many occasions that she may not want to go to college. I will admit that at first I was pretty disappointed in her.

But then I realized that she just wanted to chase another dream. From a very young age she displayed strong tendencies toward the arts and entertainment. As a seven-year-old, she began to play songs by ear and showed extreme interest in making videos and acting. I thought that these were just fun hobbies. But then I allowed her to explore her interests more and let her act and do voice-over work professionally.

She also has her own YouTube channel. I supported her by getting camera equipment, lighting, and a laptop. By the time she was eight or nine years old she was pretty proficient at creating videos, editing them, and doing graphic design. It still seems like something that she really enjoys.

In this case, because she's already showing such aptitude and diligence in arts and entertainment, I don't have a huge problem with her deciding to skip out on college. If she can prove to me that she is able to monetize her passion and turn it into a real business venture, she may do just as well or even better than had she attended college.

Another plan we've discussed is if she decides not to be in front of the camera. I've taken my kids on TV and commercial sets so they can explore all the different trades involved in film and TV production.

They get to see video editors, audio technicians, camera operators, and other types of engineers. If any one of my children were to show interest in these specific trades, they would have to have some type of training that may (or may not) include college.

Conversely, my youngest child has great aptitude in the area of mathematics and science. She enjoys her schoolwork and is an avid learner. She enjoys reading and will most likely go into a field that requires math, science, or both.

In her case, she might be a better candidate for college. She has also had some experience in acting and entertainment so she could go into some type of engineering that supports the entertainment industry or could be a paid entertainer. There are many possibilities based on my kids' interests, personalities, and aptitudes.

So as you can see, in my analysis, I am being both flexible and considering the personality of my child. You should do the same. If you've got a kid that seems like she could still make it outside of college, it could be worth having the conversation early on about how she can begin working toward her career aspirations even before college.

CHAPTER 14

Let's Talk "Post-College"

I recall, with great clarity, the process of applying for college. I remember getting several applications, composing the essays, requesting transcripts, getting teacher recommendations, and then shipping off my applications, one by one, to my top schools of choice.

I also remember completing financial aid forms and scholarship applications to help cover the cost of college. I recall getting my acceptance letters, then beaming with pride as I toted around the one I cherished most. After that, I remember going to college, taking (and missing) classes, going to parties, studying abroad, and even doing the work to reenroll every year.

What I don't remember is having very many (if any) conversations about how I'd handle my financial life after college. In fact, I was surprised when I received my very first account statement indicating it was time to start paying back my student loan.

Sure, I had an exit interview with the financial aid office. But honestly, I cannot remember much of what was discussed. I have a vague memory of someone telling me that I'll start getting my student loan bills six months after graduating. I don't remember any discussion about amounts or even the total amount of money that I owed.

Perhaps because I had private loans, I was just getting a courtesy reminder from the school so my financial life wouldn't be in shambles as an alum from there. I can't say exactly what happened, but I don't remember much information or guidance upon graduating.

You can imagine the horror that I experienced when I learned that the private student loan company that financed my college education now wanted a little over $300 per month so that I could repay the loan balance.

As I mentioned, I was working in computer sales making a cool $25,000 per year. Just a few weeks after starting the job, I signed a lease to share an apartment with a roommate. I also got a car note to round out the post-college financial disaster cocktail.

I soon learned by observing my peers and coworkers that I had probably made a couple of big financial mistakes. I saw many of them staying with their parents and driving old beat-up cars without car notes.

Instead of doing what some of my more financially savvy counterparts did, I decided that I needed the full post-college experience. I wanted to prove that I was an adult and could do grown-up things like having an apartment and owning a car.

Essentially, it was this financial behavior that nearly broke me. I was in sales and never made a lot in commission, so my salary stayed pretty low. However, the rent, my car note, and my student loan bills remained the same—high.

Eventually, I ended up quitting my job out of misery and moving in with my grandmother so I could live rent-free and pick up some of the pieces of my financial life. It was an extremely humbling experience, but it was necessary to hit the reset button and figure out how I would rebound financially.

Soon after moving in with Granny, I got married. Between my income and my husband's income, things started looking up for me financially. It took a long time to get there because I wasn't earning money right away and we were both knee-deep in student loan debt and other debt. But eventually it worked out for us.

And though it's easy for me to feel bad that this is how my financial life after college started, I'm willing to bet that many of you reading this probably had a similar story. For this reason, I think it's even more important that we talk with our daughters about what their post-college life will look like from a financial perspective.

Though we are saving money for our kids' college education, it is my hope that they will attend college very inexpensively—either through programs like dual enrollment, getting scholarships, or some other form of low-cost education. If this is the case, the money that was saved for college could be used to either purchase a home outright or serve as a significant down payment for a property.

Think about it—the reason why college is pushed on young kids is because, as many people assume, it's supposed to increase their earning power so that they can attain a certain quality of life. With a college education, you should be able to get a certain job so that you can afford the house that you want, the car that you desire, the vacations you like to take, etc.—right? Also keep in mind that that a college education adds a lot more to your life than just making more money. At the same time, if your child's interests or aptitudes lie in fields that don't require a college education, then why not use that money to jump-start them in that path?

Here's a crazy thought. What if you actually used your college money to boost your wealth-building journey through property or business ownership? Business ownership and especially property ownership can serve as a foundation for wealth-building early on in life.

In the case that you're able to start the clock on the property appreciation sooner than later, you can use the property as a way to earn income. For example, if you get roommates or rent out a unit of a duplex, you can begin building equity in a property with the help of other people's income.

With this approach, you have a chance to attain your preferred lifestyle without the large amount of unsecured debt that comes with a college education. In this scenario, you could free up more cash to pursue the quality of life that you desire—whether or not you get that dream job based on your four-year degree. If your lifestyle preferences are independent of your job prospects, you'll have more freedom to live your life on your own terms. This could be having piles of cash or it could be occupying your time with deep, meaningful work. A "preferred lifestyle" looks different for everyone, but the point is having the freedom to forge your path because you've put in the work to decrease your expenses wherever possible.

(We'll talk more about homeownership later in the book; I just wanted to drop that little nugget you're are ready to absorb it later on. Foregoing college in order to be a homeowner is a novel concept, so I mention it a few times in the book for your full consideration!)

In an ideal world, I am hoping that my girls are able to get through college inexpensively and use their money to start building wealth early on. Of course, at the end of the day, the money that we've saved for them is there to do what they please with it. However, I'm hoping that we can reverse the trend of crippling student loan debt among our female demographic.

There can be a better way to handle post-college life so that our daughters are not financially strapped. If they can be property owners (ideally income-generating property) sooner than later, I think it's worth exploring.

If that's not an option, then the conversation should revolve around how they will reduce their living expenses to prioritize debt repayment and begin the investing and wealth-building journey sooner than later.

As we saw in the investing chapter, time equals money, so starting right away is crucial. If you can talk about the benefits of being able to invest aggressively and with sizable amounts of money early on, then you can help your daughter cut down the length of her working career dramatically.

If you are able to put considerable amounts of income away into savings each year, it can cut your active working career down by 10, 20, or even 30 years. For example, a 21-year-old who is able to save half of her income until the age of 31 might be at that point ready to get married and start to have children. It would be a perfect time to press pause on a working career for those reasons. It would be even more perfect if there's a financial cushion to support that decision.

What your daughter does after college matters. That's why I think it's important to talk about how your daughter can live as frugally as possible or earn as much money as possible, or both. With this outlook, she'll have plenty of income to put toward paying off debt, investing, savings, business ownership, and property ownership.

The next conversation you should have is around student loans and other debt. Hopefully, you're having this discussion with your daughter before she even starts her college career and makes the decision to take on debt. If you're having this conversation after student debt has already entered the picture, you can still effectively talk about how to tackle that debt.

There are a lot of opinions when it comes to paying down debt. Some people believe that low-interest debt is okay to keep around. The idea here is that you can either put your money in investments that offer a greater return than the interest you'll pay on debt or have a higher quality of life (i.e. use your excess funds to support your lifestyle).

I've actually talked to some people who have already determined that they will never pay off their student loan debt. It's just not appealing to them because they believe that there are better things that they can do with their money. That, coupled with the idea that this type of debt does not get passed down to dependents or heirs, makes people feel secure about student loan debt and other types of debt around.

Though there is no one right way to do this, I would caution against this approach. For one, we actually don't know what will happen to all of this federally subsidized student loan debt. The rules are ever-changing and the penalties for taking longer to pay seem to be increasing.

For example, your income tax refund check could be seized if you've got delinquent student loans. In some cases, your professional license and even driver's license could be revoked![1] And these were all things that no one thought would come down the pipeline.

Though you might be depending on certain laws that protect you as a borrower, the fact of the matter is you don't know when or if these things can change or if carrying student loan debt could present some serious limitations to your life as a free citizen.

For this reason, I am a fan of paying off student loan debt as soon as possible. The wild card is the federal government, and we just don't know what they'll do and how they'll deal with student loan debt 10, 20, or 30 years down the line.

In terms of other debt, it probably will be higher interest rate debt. In this case, the high interest rate on this type of debt could negate any gains that you would make in the stock market or with other investments.

Now, there are exceptions to this rule. For example, if you have some type of startup or you're able to turn small amounts of money into an extremely large amount of money, then of course it makes sense to put your money where it grows and outpaces high-interest debt. With the large majority of people, this will not be the case.

If you don't have some multimillion-dollar startup or some other money-making machine, it's in your best interest to pay off other debt as well. Because again, here we have another wild card. You don't know when or if disaster or tragedy could strike, causing you to be delinquent on debt obligations.

You could lose your job, fall ill, or become temporarily or permanently disabled. You may just have a desire to go on vacation or attend your best friend's wedding. In all these cases, you may not be able to or want to service the high-interest debt that you are now obligated to pay.

---

1   Rakoczy, Christy. "Got Unpaid Student Loans? You Could Lose Your License In These States." Student Loan Hero, September 18, 2019. https://studentloan hero.com/featured/unpaid-student-loans-facing-default-lose-license-states/.

If you can't tell, I truly believe that paying down debt of any kind should be prioritized immediately after college. This financial focus will impact things like your daughter's living situation and other expenses that she decides to take on (or not take on.)

As you discuss all of these possibilities and eventualities, I can bet that your daughter, with her know-it-all attitude, will retort with a clever reply like, "Well, Mom, that might have been *your* story or that might be Susie-save-a-lot's story, but that won't be me." Depending on her maturity level, she probably still has a pretty unrealistic view of the world and could possibly maintain that until after college.

She might insist (like I did with my mother) that she is differ-ent and that she is more of a genius than anyone else. She might be smarter or prettier or more popular, etc., so post-college poverty could not possibly happen to her.

In some cases this could be true. Especially, if your daughter decides to go into some type of technical discipline that tends to pay higher like engineering, life sciences, medicine, law, or any other higher-paying field. For the rest of us, there is a high chance that the student loan debt may not justify our career choice.

We know this is true, due to the $1.5 trillion student loan crisis that millions of Americans are dealing with. But in the event that your daughter doesn't believe numbers, statistics, or documented evidence, you may be able to convince her to make a sensible post-college plan after all. This little exercise might open her eyes to what her post-col-lege life could look like.

If you did that activity in the last chapter where your daughter found her potential salary from the US Department of Labor Statistics, she should have found some key data points like how fast her career path or chosen profession is growing along with the average salaries for those professions.

Once you have this in place, it's time to start outlining a post-college budget. This will be fun for your daughter because this is where she gets to paint an exciting picture on the canvas of her mind about how grown up an adult she'll be after college.

Ask her what kind of car she'll want to drive; where she'll want to live; and how much she'll spend on clothing, food, utilities, and other living expenses. From the last chapter, you should have already looked up her school choices and tuition costs. From here, you can extrapolate loan numbers and an estimated monthly payment amount. (Check out this student loan repayment calculator[2] if you need help getting real numbers.)

Add those student loan payments to her post-college budget so that she can see the numbers for herself. Just as she was excited to write down her car of choice and the fabulous high-rise condo she'll be living in in Miami or LA, she'll be forced to look at the figures when it comes to her salary and her student loan debt versus her desired lifestyle.

Again, she may not concede that your line of reasoning or your way of thinking about minimizing debt sooner than later makes sense right away. At the very least, you've planted the seeds that may help her make decisions about (1) the college she will attend, (2) her career choice, (3) whether or not she'll be willing to take on student loan debt, and (4) how she'll conduct her financial affairs after college.

After looking at the real numbers and the figures she may decide to attend a less expensive college to avoid student loan debt. She may even ask for permission to stay with you while she pays off debt and drives your used car!

Of course, this is an ideal outcome. I cannot make any promises, but I do think it's a valuable exercise to help bring your daughter to reality when it comes to planning her life right after college.

---

2 "Repayment Estimator." Repayment Calculator | Federal Student Loans. Accessed November 13, 2019. https://studentloans.gov/myDirectLoan/repay mentEstimator.action.

CHAPTER 15

Let's Talk Career and Income

In the previous chapter, we talked about what post-college life might look like for your daughter. A lot of what we addressed pertains to how to live frugally and cut expenses so that wealth-building can start sooner in her life.

As mentioned previously, women will typically earn less than men in their lifetimes due to a number of factors that include the gender wage gap as well as the time young women may take off to start and raise a family. One should also consider the longer lifespan of women, which might require them to actually save more than their male counterparts.

When it comes to talking about how to level the field for your daughter, this might be one of the most intense conversations you'll have with her. After all, you want the best for her and your hope is that by having attended college and pursuing the career of dreams, she'll be financially stable enough to live the lifestyle that you always wanted for your little princess.

For me, I just knew that I would be a millionaire by the tender young age of 21. I didn't have a plan, or any million-dollar skills to draw from, but I still had a strong belief that millionaire status was well within my reach. As of this writing, I'm 39 and while I'm not doing terrible for myself, my husband and I still have a little ways to go before we reach millionaire status.

What's more is that millionaire status isn't even what it used to be. You can own a few properties, have a decently funded retirement savings account, and by the time you turn 40, 50, or definitely 60 years old, you *should* be able to be a millionaire.

In other words, owning a couple of houses worth $250,000 a piece plus $500,000 in retirement account makes you a millionaire. That breakdown makes millionaire status well within reach nowadays, but the sad part is that many Americans are sorely behind when it comes to saving for retirement and building their net worth.

I say all of this only to point out that (1) millionaire status is possible, but (2) it's not that possible if you don't have a concrete plan to get there. A large part of that plan will have to do with the income you make, the lifestyle you sustain, and what you do with your excess funds. Ideally, you'll want to encourage your daughter to create a large gap (in the positive) between her living expenses and her income.

Honestly, the easy part is being Frugal Fannie. After all, there are plenty of shows out there that highlight the lives and endeavors of extreme couponers and cheapskates. Cutting back seems so much more within reach for the average American. Tell someone that all their financial problems will be solved if they just make two million dollars per year, and the viewership of those exciting reality shows would soon plummet!

Cutting back on expenses and lifestyle is a great start to the path of financial freedom but there's a point where innovation and increasing income becomes paramount. It can be hard to make the shift from a thrifty mindset to an abundance mindset but it's necessary to lay a strong foundation for financial independence. After all, if somebody came to you and demanded that you figure out how to earn $1 million or $2 million by next year, what would be your plan to do so?

Would you wallow in self-pity complaining about how unfair life is? Or would you get super creative, hunker down, and figure out how to get it done? The mindset that we adopt around making more money, increasing income, and building wealth will be the same mindset we relay to our daughters.

For this reason, we must choose wisely what side of the fence we'll be on. We can choose to continue embracing a poverty mentality or we can demonstrate to our daughters that the sky's the limit. Whether we think they are or not, they are watching!

As you might have guessed already, I fall into the latter camp. I'm still figuring out how to make that cool million this year, but you better believe that I'm still working on it. I believe it can be done and I want my daughters to see me working toward the goals of increasing our income.

With this in mind, I think there are great ways to frame a conversation around increasing income and even optimizing the money that comes into your daughter's hands throughout the course of her working career.

(Remember, if you are talking to teenagers or even young adults, you may not be able to convince them to see your point of view right away. As I've advocated throughout the entire book, the idea is just to start the conversations to plant seeds that could ultimately turn into a better financial outcome for our daughters.)

Earning More Money in a Job Before Going Out on Your Own

All the cool kids are starting businesses these days. And while I am a huge proponent of starting a business, it's not for everyone all the time.

While it is "sexy" to be a business owner, CEO, or general highfalutin shot caller, there will be a time when you'll have to learn something from someone. You may need to work a regular job until you are disciplined enough to launch your own company. You may need to stash a cash cushion to support your future business efforts. This takes time and it happens in various stages of life.

These are all good reasons to experience some time in corporate America or in a nine-to-five job before you jump-start your career as a business owner. Many people pursue business ownership prematurely and they haven't mastered basic financial principles like decreasing their personal burn rate (i.e. personal expenditures and cost of living), saving, budgeting, or just being responsible with their money.

Though I would not discourage my daughters to start a business, I would talk to them realistically about the proficiency they have demonstrated when it comes to handling their personal finances and how that could affect their business competencies. If they don't understand basic business concepts like profitability, negotiation, or building a team, one of the best ways to get this experience might be working for someone else for a time.

Yes, the Internet memes tell us, "Why work hard building someone else's dreams when you could be building your own?" But a desire to start a business doesn't necessarily qualify someone to do that.

Experience can be an excellent teacher, but if you can get someone to pay for your experience, why not get it on someone else's dime? A perk is that you can be saving money to finance your entrepreneurship efforts down the road as well.

When I graduated college and lost out on what would have been a fairly lucrative pharmaceutical sales representative job and instead went into computer sales, I was devastated. I felt like I was struggling to meet my goals in the midst of a good old boy network that I had no desire or probably even ability to join and move up the ranks. I was miserable.

However, there was a valuable skill that I learned there that would help me build a sales and marketing consultancy that eventually turned into a profitable database consulting operation. In computer sales, I learned the art of cold-calling and sending cold emails to generate leads. We had a goal to make upwards of one hundred calls per day. The people who consistently hit those effort numbers were the ones who typically made their sales goals.

In addition to making cold calls, we had to schedule follow-up activity with prospects in a software known as a customer relationship manager (CRM). It was here that I learned the art of picking up the phone to cold-call people and how to follow up in a systematic way to generate sales. Though much of the time I was pretty unmotivated when it came to hitting my call numbers, that skill and method of operation enabled me to hire, train, and track other salespeople in small businesses.

Because of my brief stint in corporate America, I was able to start my own company that provided extremely effective sales and marketing consulting along with database implementation for small sales departments. In some cases, I was able to help my clients double their company's revenue in just 12 to 18 months!

The one thing I wish I did was take advantage of some of the financial benefits available to me while I worked my corporate job. If I had stuck it out, I probably would have begun making my sales numbers with consistency. I would have made enough money to participate in the employee stock option purchase program and even the 401(k) plan. Sadly, I was still pretty much living check to check, drowning in student loans and other expenses, and barely saved any money for the day that I quit brashly to pursue business ownership.

But it doesn't have to be this way for our daughters. The truth of the matter is that people are obligated to work 30 years or more because we subscribe to excessive consumerism. As I mentioned in the last chapter, a working career doesn't have to be 30 years if we are wise with our income.

To this end, I do encourage my daughters, if they decide to be traditionally employed, to take advantage of any financial benefits like flexible spending accounts, health savings accounts, employer-sponsored retirement plans, and even stock option purchase opportunities.

While encouraging our daughters to take advantage of the benefits of full-time employment, we can still give them hope that full-time employment doesn't have to last forever. Traditional employment really can be a foundation for other dreams they may have in their hearts like traveling the world, starting a business, or even raising a family.

Here are some tips that can make your daughter's employment years both enjoyable and productive.

Do Something You Enjoy

Should your daughter have to submit herself to the "drudgery" of the nine-to-five, the ideal thing to do would be something that she enjoys. That should also be balanced out with a position that pays well or has the potential to pay well over time.

Unpaid internships can be a great way to break into high-paying yet competitive industries or job positions. When you get into fields like television/film, advertising, fashion, and related artsy professions, it can take a long time to climb to the top. There are plenty of people who started as interns and eventually rose through the ranks to become extremely high-paid executives or decision-makers in these fields.

While statistics are somewhat unclear on the issue of how this approach pans out for most people, I think there can be a smart way to take on the free internship route provided there is a clear path to a paid position along with the potential for upward mobility. Promotion can happen, but it will simply take some research, networking, and grinding. If your daughter has a personality that works for this approach, this could be a great way to get into a field that is enjoyable yet lucrative.

On the flip side, internships that are very low-paying positions in "exciting" competitive careers can also become time-sucking black holes that never go anywhere. Make sure that your daughter has a well-thought-out game plan with contingencies and backups in the case that her dream career or position doesn't materialize as soon as she thought.

Ideally, the no- to low-paying internship can work if you've got money or some other resources (like a trust fund, inexpensive housing, or other financial support). If you've been able to save money so that your daughter can pursue things that interest her, this would be an ideal scenario.

If you haven't saved up any money or can't provide substantial financial support, this might be a good time to have that conversation about saving up for a car versus saving up for a career opportunity. If you know that your daughter is eyeing one of these competitive fields, you'll want to talk with her, early on, about how you could possibly support her (or how she could support herself) should she come across this type of opportunity.

I mentioned the internship strategy because something enjoyable may not always be the highest paid career opportunity—in the beginning. For others, their preferred profession may actually offer a decent salary with benefits to boot. If this is the case, great! Your daughter could be on the path to a very fulfilling career in a company and profession that she enjoys. That's definitely a win-win.

Then, there is the possibility that your daughter already has her eyes on a shortened working career. She feels as though she is disciplined enough to save a substantial amount of her earnings and expects to be done working in 10 to 15 years (which, again, is totally doable with the right financial strategy).

In this case, she might have the tolerance for a little bit of "nine-to-five drudgery" because she knows that it is short-term. She might be okay with a more technical, tedious career even though it's not what she's totally passionate about. However, the pay might be high enough so that she can live on a small amount of her income and exit the obligatory working years at her leisure.

A good thing to talk about with your daughter is what she could see herself doing even if she didn't get paid for it. That will give you insight into what she enjoys and help you all brainstorm career paths that have a good intersection between her personality, skill set, competitiveness, and desired compensation.

From here, you should be able to get a good idea of what type of work, lifestyle, and even outcomes that she expects from her working professional career. If you're having this conversation during her pre-teen years, it could even help you choose her courses for high school and college so that she's right on track early on.

Find a Job and Company Culture That Fits You

Another option is to encourage your daughter to find a totally awesome company culture that works for her. No, she may not be terribly passionate about accounting, but she may be extremely passionate about a company that "gets" her.

Maybe casual Fridays isn't just a Friday thing or she's able to bring her dog to the office. The company policy might allow her to take time off for volunteer work or they might give a sizable portion of their profits to charity.

In this "perfect company" scenario, she may like that there are no walls or cubicles and that collaboration between departments and coworkers is facilitated through open-door policies or even frequent interdepartmental meetings. Maybe she just appreciates the free bagels on Tuesdays.

Even if it's a career that may not be her final destination or capture her heart to the utmost, it can help to be working for a great company. Encourage your daughter that she shouldn't fear being too selective when it comes to choosing an employer.

She should be ready to interview them as much as they are ready to interview her. Let her know that she can ask her prospective interviewer where they see their company going in the next 5 to 10 years and how a position like hers can fit into that vision. She should feel comfortable asking about opportunities for advancement and inquiring about the nature of the company culture.

This line of questioning proves that she's really looking for the best fit possible. She's not just looking for any job, but rather a position that's made for her in a company that's right for her. Employers will appreciate that, and it may even give her a leg up in the interview process.

She should also know that it's okay to say no to a position. Even though the money looks good and the opportunity may seem perfect, if her gut tells her otherwise, go ahead and listen. She could avoid heartache and trouble by declining a position at a company that isn't the best fit for her.

Finally, she might feel like she's a good fit for a company, but maybe the position itself isn't right for her. Again, she should go with her gut and be okay with saying no to a position that might not be in her wheelhouse. If she feels like the company is a great fit but the position isn't, she may even be able to "pitch" the idea that another position better suited for her skill set and experience be created for her.

The point here is to be flexible and think of other ways that employment can serve her, and vice versa. Of course, employees are paid to do well for their employers, but in order for that to happen, your daughter has to be sure that she is in a great environment with a position that suits her. Let her know, don't be afraid to seek that out and get what she desires. After all, if she is going to spend a lot of time and dedicate herself to a job and position, it better be something that's a good fit.

Show Up and Do Your Best

If she does decide to work for an employer until she can launch her own venture, make sure that she makes a personal commitment to be the very best version of herself she can be on the job. It's not enough just to show up, a point you should emphasize with her.

After all, one never knows what those job connections could turn into. A coworker could end up being a prized business partner. A supervisor could become her first and most profitable client. Someone in HR could help her find great talent for her soon-to-be business.

After all, she doesn't want to be known as the slacker or the difficult person at work. She should want people to know that she is a person of integrity and that if she is called on to handle a task or project, she will do her best to get it done.

It's not wise to burn bridges just because you think you won't be at a job for a long time. Even in the most adverse circumstances, your daughter should make up her mind to do her very best because the connections and the skills that she gathers there should serve her well when she does eventually jump-start her own venture.

Keep a Record of Your Accomplishments

An employer may already have a system in place to track progress and accomplishments. If this is so, make sure there's a way that your daughter can keep this information for herself as a record.

If there's nothing in place to track these things for her, she should create her own. She could create a folder in her email box that highlights customer testimonials or goals that she made for herself, and in turn accomplished.

If possible, she should try to keep a journal or some type of record of things that she does from day to day and week to week. If she accomplishes something big or small, encourage her to keep a record of it because it will come in handy when she applies for a new position, has performance reviews, or anyone calls into question what exactly she does in her job or what she has accomplished.

Ask for a Raise

Hopefully, your daughter's employer has some type of review process in place to confirm her excellent performance.

Quarterly or annual reviews can serve to help her become even better at what she does. The review process should point out things that she is good at along with those in areas of development. She should also be able to see how she's improved as an employee.

Another great thing that can happen at review time is that she becomes eligible for a raise. Some employers already have a set percentage in terms of raise amounts, and others may depend on the employee to ask for a percentage or negotiate a raise.

Even if it looks like there is a set percentage in place, I like to encourage girls to try to negotiate something higher. Encourage your daughter to ask for more than she expects so that if her employer negotiates, it may eventually land on the amount that she wanted in the first place.

Tip: if your daughter actually gets a raise, she should plan to divert it toward savings instead of increasing her expenses. The more money she saves earlier in her career, the faster she could potentially retire or leave to pursue her own thing. I'm just going to keep saying this: with saving and investing, time equals money! So emphasize the importance of using those raises and increases in pay for investing and saving.

Establish Comradery and Connections

Since we are talking about our daughters, we should also address the inevitable—the tendency for women to get catty and petty on the job. Encourage your daughters to participate in *healthy* competition that makes them better at what they do. Also, make sure that same ambition is tempered with a tendency to collaborate and connect with the women around them.

When women get together to collaborate, connect, and cooperate, some amazing things can happen. We must be mindful to teach our daughters how to deescalate situations with other women who are not familiar with the new code of conduct we are trying to establish among this young sisterhood.

Offenses will come, gossip will be spoken, and nasty attitudes will be copped. These are things that happen when women work together. But we can talk to our daughters about changing that. This is a great time to start discussing teamwork and being the bigger person when these issues rear their ugly heads.

Teach them that strife and contention is not always about them personally and that it can often be a reflection of what someone else is going through. Let's teach them that even when people are mean and nasty, they may have to turn the other cheek and show a different side of themselves.

When it comes to women dealing with women, we must be softer, kinder, and more patient with each other. It's a tall order, but it'll make work and friendships in life overall much easier for our daughters in the workplace.

CHAPTER 16

Let's Talk Starting a Business

Women are among the fastest growing demographic of people starting businesses. We live in such a great time in history where it's incredibly easy to start and grow a business.

Even if you don't know how to do something perfectly, there are tons of resources online to help you learn how to do pretty much anything— from crafting, to programming, to video production, and even accounting—there's just so many things that can be done to start a business.

Because it is so easy to start a business these days, however, the low barrier-to-entry makes it a very competitive landscape out there. But that doesn't mean we should discourage our daughters from trying to get a piece of the business pie.

There are many ways that our daughters can differentiate themselves and actually be successful in business. One of the best ways is having sufficient capital to invest in business activities to start and sustain a profitable operation.

This is why it's okay for your daughter to work a traditional job at first. By working, she amasses valuable skills that can serve her and her entrepreneurship journey. She should also be saving money as she's traditionally employed.

In actuality, money can help her stand out from the rest in business. This is not to discount the bootstrapped businesses, but having enough money to really invest in a business can make all the difference.

How Can I Help My Daughter Pick a Business Idea?

Perhaps one of the most difficult things today is getting our young people to focus. After all, there are so many opportunities, and the Internet is full of success stories and ways to make money. Your daughter may be one of those people that can do several things well. In order to succeed in business, she just needs to focus on one.

Yes, we all know about multiple streams of income, but the stream of income that comes from one's talent and expertise should be built first. Beyond that, the profits that come in from that "one excellent thing" can go into more passive types of income like real estate, securities, royalties, etc. The key is finding the main focus that creates enough cashflow to sustain one's lifestyle and then eventually other streams of income.

While helping your daughter focus on a business idea, show her how to take stock of things that she enjoys along with things that she is good at. Ask her questions like:

- What do people say you do better than anyone else?
- Of all the skills/resources you possess, which ones do you think are the most developed?
- Of all the skills/resources you possess, which ones do you think can be turned into a business?
- How much money do you have to start your business?
- How much time do you have to start your business?

In many cases, your daughter will probably have ample time and little money in the beginning stages of her working career or business-building journey. It's at this point that you might want to suggest she start with freelancing or something service-based to start building capital (if she doesn't have it).

These kinds of businesses can still be profitable and they are not normally capital-intensive. The goal here is to get your daughter to start working for herself and then funneling those earnings into her own business idea.

An example of this might be starting a restaurant. Restaurants are extremely capital-intensive, and the failure rate for them is pretty high. Sinking $250,000 into a restaurant may not be the best idea for a young woman with no business experience.

For these business ideas, I suggest the "dream snowball." With the dream snowball, you can start with a smaller, less capital-intensive version of your dream and build it up as you're able to make it grow.

Your daughter may not have money to start a restaurant business, but she may have money to become a food blogger. Maybe she has the time and the equipment to post videos of herself making recipes or tasting new and exciting foods on YouTube or Instagram.

If she can figure out a way to monetize those activities, she can take those earnings and put them into a catering business. Catering businesses are beneficial because one can determine exactly how much food one needs and waste is minimalized in this model. The predictability lends itself to a leaner, more profitable operation as far as food service goes.

Once the catering business is successful, she can look into restaurant pop-ups or a food truck. If those are successful, it could be time to look for a space and actually open that restaurant. This is just one example of the snowball method of opening and starting a business.

Maybe your daughter wants to start a travel and tour business. Those are not terribly capital-intensive, but if she doesn't get enough people to sign up for the trips, she could end up losing money if she's already forked over a deposit. With things like Airbnb Experiences and the Internet in general, she can create meetups and small tour groups to "snowball" that business into a full-scale travel and tour business.

I think you get the point here. If there's not a lot of money to start with, that doesn't mean that your daughter can't start the business of her dreams. It just might mean she'll have to work a little bit harder and start a little bit *before* scratch to get going on her business dream.

How Can My Daughter Finance Her Business?

We already discussed the option of using the dream snowball, which is a form of bootstrapping a business. But there are other ways to finance a business.

One way to start a business is to raise money. This could be done via crowdfunding, approaching friends and family, or even going the startup route by raising equity over several rounds of raising capital.

Depending on your personal network, these financial routes could be difficult. However, I wouldn't take this form of financing off the table, as there are many women who have founded successful startups by raising money from friends and family, going the startup route with Angel Investors, or even participating in business incubators and accelerators.

Founders like Tara Reed of Apps Without Code[1] went the accelerator route to start her business while Georgene Huang of Fairygodboss was able to raise millions of dollars for her startup. Crowdfunding platform, Indiegogo, reports that 47 percent of successful fundraising campaigns are run by women.[2]

---

1   Walravens, Samantha. "How to Succeed in Silicon Valley When You Don't Look Like Mark Zuckerberg." Forbes. Forbes Magazine, April 8, 2017. https://www.forbes.com/sites/geekgirlrising/2017/04/07/5-startup-tips-from-a-black-female-non-technical-founder/.

2   "A Celebration of Female Entrepreneurs on Indiegogo." Indiegogo. Accessed November 13, 2019. https://www.indiegogo.com/campaign_collections/a-celebration-of-female-entrepreneurs.

Another way to raise money for a business is to use credit cards. This is not ideal, but in some circumstances it could actually work out. If your daughter is able to get special introductory rate offers with low or no interest, and have a clear path to profitability, then credit card use could be an option.

However with this approach, your daughter needs to understand that it is a huge risk that if things go wrong, she could be on the hook for thousands of dollars of credit card debt. Credit card interest rates are very high and the interest compounds quickly on high balances.

If your daughter is set on using credit cards to finance her business, she should try to start with a small credit card with a goal of paying it off right away. For example, if she has a retail business and she knows that she will be able to buy X number of units and then turn around and sell them for Y amount of dollars in a short period of time, a low-interest credit card could work.

If your daughter is brand-spanking-new to her business and doesn't have enough data to prove her path-to-profitability hypothesis, then credit cards might not be the best way to start.

Personal loans are a growing financial product that many people are using to finance things like vacations, small home repairs, consolidating high-interest debt, and even starting businesses. Personal loans tend to have slightly lower interest rates than credit cards. But because it's unsecured debt, they can be hard to qualify for.

Next up are bank loans, which can be extremely difficult to get, especially for a new business. Most of the time, banks extend credit to business owners and businesses that have an established history of profitable operation. These loans could also require a considerable amount of collateral plus a personal pledge by the owner to guarantee the loan.

For this reason, new business owners don't usually start with these kinds of loans. The qualifications are extremely strict and the likelihood of your daughter meeting the criteria is slim as a new business owner.

Another way to finance a business is simply by using cash. We discussed this option already, but if your daughter has been working on a job or if she's been saving her money for quite some time, then using cash to finance her business could help her avoid going into debt. If the business doesn't do well right away or at all, she's only out of cash and not indebted to credit card companies.

Borrowing From a 401(k)

If your daughter doesn't have any cash handy, there is another way to finance her business. She could borrow from a retirement savings account like a 401(k). Though I highly advise against the strategy, I still bring it up because (1) it's something that someone will probably suggest to your daughter one day anyway, so you might as well preemptively talk about it—both the good and the bad—and, (2) in some cases, it could be a valid strategy in helping finance a fledgling business.

Using a 401(k) loan can be risky because the penalties for non-repayment can be high. For instance, if you take out a 401(k) loan and your employment is severed, you must pay back the loan by the due date of your tax return for the year in which the distribution occurs.

If you don't make that deadline, you'll be hit with a 10 percent early-withdrawal penalty by the IRS. Also, the outstanding balance of the loan is treated as a taxable distribution and your employer will then report the distribution to the IRS. This could bump you into another tax bracket and cause you to owe even more money to the IRS.

On the other side, these loans can be extremely low interest and if you have a plan to pay it off very quickly, then it could be exactly what you need to get your business going. After all, it's your money that you took time to save and put away, so you should have access to it. The only issue is that because you paid into this account with pre-tax money, you'll get heavily penalized for not paying it back.

I will say that this is a tool that we have utilized personally to finance some real estate ventures. It's not something you want to depend on all the time, though. When we use this strategy, it's with the goal of paying off the loan right away.

The few times that we did take out a 401(k) loan, we actually expedited the payments because keeping that kind of loan was just too risky for us. Fortunately, it worked out every time, but I know other people who weren't so fortunate.

If your daughter is starting the right kind of business that ends up being profitable, this should only be a stepping stone in her business financing strategy. In the end, she'll have to make a decision on the business financing method that works well for her.

Should I Invest in My Daughter's Dream?

I believe it's every mother's dream to invest in their daughter to the utmost. We take time off when they are born. Some of us stay home to raise them until they are school-age, and there are even others that complete the journey by homeschooling them through high school.

We stay up with them to do homework. We find tutors for them. We look for the best schools. We try to give them the very best of us so that they can have the very best of life.

Whatever sacrifices we've made definitely count as an investment into our daughter's future. But whether or not it's a good idea for a mom or another family member to invest in a relative's business will be entirely up to your family.

Things between friends, family, and money can get pretty sticky if the terms aren't spelled out clearly. Even when terms are clear, things can still go awry when you mix family and money. Emotions get involved and relationships can be ruined. However, some really beautiful, wonderful things and businesses can come out of families putting their resources together. Some of the most successful businesses in the world are small family-owned, closely-held companies.

Investing in your daughter's business could be a perfect way to establish a generational legacy of wealth. Before you say yes though, I would suggest that you ask a few questions and have a deep discussion with your daughter to make sure everyone's on the same page when it comes to going into business together. Here are some questions to ask yourself and discuss with your daughter as you analyze your choice:

- What will be the nature of our partnership? Will I give my daughter money? Will I give her mentorship support?
- How is the relationship between myself and my daughter? Is it strained? Is it healthy? If I invest money in my daughter's business and lose it all, would that be a problem for me? Would my daughter feel guilty?
- Does my daughter have a solid business plan and/or track record of success in the industry she's operating in?
- Does my daughter display qualities that make her a competent business owner? If she doesn't yet possess the skills and experience for business, does she have the connections to hire the people that she needs to be successful?
- If I can't give money, what are other ways I can invest in my daughter's business?

Be clear about your personal goals when it comes to investing in your daughter's business. If it's moral support, make sure your investment is on par with that goal. If you truly believe this could make you both filthy rich, communicate that with your daughter so that she understands what you desire out of the financial partnership you'll have in the business.

Evaluating the Business Success

A wise man once said, "If it don't make dollars, it don't make sense." Being in business can be fun and prestigious, but the numbers must make sense or it's a hobby.

Imagine your daughter is able to start a successful freelance photography business, but it seems that she is still living paycheck-to-paycheck. Think about your other daughter who's able to sell leather goods on Etsy. She's making hundreds of thousands of dollars a year in revenue but has no health insurance or retirement plan to speak of.

This is a phenomenon called entrepreneurial poverty. This happens when people are so passionate about their business that they really can't see the forest for the trees. And though there is often a period of time when businesses won't be profitable, eventually a business should not only be able to take care of the owner but other people as well. Sadly, I've seen far too many people, especially women, put their all into their business and get virtually nothing back.

With this in mind, I encourage you to talk about entrepreneurial poverty with your daughter. It might look like she is living her dream and really doing something she's passionate about. But if her basic needs cannot be meant, then her business is not really a business. It's an expensive, gut-wrenching, draining hobby that needs to be replaced by a real business or real business systems in order to support the owner's lifestyle.

In some cases, this happens because again it's really not a business. Nevertheless, in other cases, it really does come down to your daughter's level of understanding in terms of managing business resources.

Being able to allocate money that comes towards budget expenses like 401(k) savings, health insurance, and taxes should be a priority.

If you feel like your daughter is generally good with money but doesn't understand how to apply that to her businesses financials, a great book to check is *Profit First* by Mike Michalowicz. This book helps entrepreneurs understand how to divvy up their business earnings and better use the resources they have.

We, as women, are naturally more giving and tend to tolerate pain for longer periods of time. This can cause us to pour resources into a business that is poorly run, which eventually leads to burnout. You do not want your daughter to be stuck in the rat race of entrepreneurial poverty. You want her to have a thriving business, not glorified self-employment, that she can pass down to her own daughters or granddaughters when the time comes.

At the end of the day, entrepreneurship and small business can be a totally viable venture for your daughter. It teaches so many life lessons, plus it has the added benefit of creating uncapped income potential. We definitely need more wealthy women in the world and in leadership roles such as the ones created through profitable business ownership.

CHAPTER 17

Let's Talk Love, Dating, Marriage, and Kids

When you mix money with romance, things can get stressful pretty quickly. Studies show that 40 to 50 percent of marriages in the US end in divorce.[1] What's more is that many couples end up fighting over finances. One study says that money issues are the second-leading cause of divorce after infidelity.[2]

They say that money is the root of all evil, but this comes from I Timothy 6:10 in the Bible verse which states that the *love* of money is the root of all evil.[3] In all actuality, money is neither good nor bad.

Money simply magnifies what someone values and how they think. So you can imagine that when two people get together to sort out their money, conflicting stances regarding values and general worldviews come into play.

---

1 "Marriage & Divorce." American Psychological Association. Accessed November 13, 2019. https://www.apa.org/topics/divorce/.

2 "Money Ruining Marriages in America: A Ramsey Solutions Study." Dave Ramsey, February 7, 2018. https://www.daveramsey.com/pr/money-ruining -marriages-in-america.

3 I Timothy 6:10 (KJV).

These differences in opinions and views can lead to money squabbles and money misunderstandings. To further complicate things, there can even be different money personality types.

For instance, there can be a spender and a saver in each relationship. Sometimes, the two can pair up in a marriage partnership, but it's not often that it happens.

The spender typically likes to spend money and doesn't always value saving up money for a rainy day. The saver is much more conservative in spending. They tend to look for deals, discounts, and opportunities to stockpile money. When trying to balance these priorities in a relationship, it can get very difficult.

Before we jump into handling finances in a marriage, I think it's fair to talk about finances when it comes to what precedes marriage—relationships, dating, and courtship.

When I have this conversation with my daughters, I encourage them to date according to their values and standards. That means if they value character and integrity in a person, they should make sure the person they date does the same and lives up to those standards.

Things like character integrity will spill over into money situations, especially in a marriage. For this reason, I have warned my daughters to watch a potential mate's behavior not only when it comes to romantic relationships but also when it comes to relationships in general.

If you notice someone is willing to lie to their mother or even their boss, it means that they lack integrity. A lack of integrity can cause so many relationship problems—especially with money.

At the end of the day, if our daughters should decide to pursue marriage, it should be with someone with whom they can build a legacy. In order to build with someone, there must be similar values and standards on both sides.

Building a legacy together means you must trust each other and that you'll keep *each other's* best interest in mind. This requires operating in the utmost integrity when it comes to making decisions regarding your relationship—and that includes money decisions.

Furthermore, we should tell our daughters that how someone manages their money reveals a lot about their personal life and how they treat others. If we observe people around us mismanaging money, it means that they don't love themselves. And if they don't love themselves with *their* own money habits, how could they love anyone else effectively? It sounds like a strange connection, but it's something we should point out to our daughters (more on self-love and money later in the book).

Women tend to see the good and the potential in someone—especially when it comes to young men they are involved with. I believe that can be a good thing. As long as a man has a dream as well as a vision of how to achieve that dream and a plan of execution, I think he deserves the support that a young woman can give him in a marriage. (Let's face it, dating relationships can be so temporary that investing the time and energy to help build someone's dream could be a waste. But that's my two cents.)

However, a man who doesn't have a clear vision of his personal development journey may not have clear standards and boundaries regarding much in his life. (Of course, the same can go for women, but we are discussing the money conversations we're having with our daughters.) If this is true, then there could be a huge potential for money issues in the relationship. If someone doesn't commit to being responsible and integrous with money, there are other holes in their character that can present problems in a marriage later on.

Of course, we don't want to train our daughters to ask during a first date, "What's your net worth and how much money do you make and what's your debt to income ratio?" That' s a little too straightforward. Or as they say these days, "Too much too soon."

But we do want to train them to observe people in all relationships, especially those that can turn romantic and eventually develop into marriage. As you train them to observe, they should take note how their potential mate treats a server when they go out to eat. How do they tip that server?

Look at the way they treat their subordinates or talk about their superiors. How do they interact with people in their families? Do they have bill collectors blowing up their phone 24 hours a day? Do they have overdue bill notices piling up? Not that these things mean our daughters should immediately walk away, but if they are happening is there a plan to remedy them? Just being observant can save your daughter a world of heartache and drama later on.

There will come a time when it's totally appropriate to begin having money conversations in a romantic relationship. If this relationship is decidedly going towards marriage, money should come up at some point. In fact, it might be a series of conversations that your daughter should have with her mate.

When my husband and I knew that we were on track to get married, we began to talk about finances. I began to disclose to him the amount of student loan debt that I had along with the plans that I had to pay it off.

Even though I was hardly making any money at the time, he seemed convinced of my plan. I even shared with him my dream to be totally and utterly debt-free one day. It wasn't long before he felt comfortable sharing his financial status with me, too. He told me about the amount of student loans that he (thought) he had and we talked about the different ways we could tackle it.

As I mentioned in my money story, my husband underestimated his student loan debt by about $20,000. Shortly, after we got married, one of those student loan companies started to garnish his wages, so we felt the effect of it pretty quickly.

Needless to say, it was a bumpy start to our marriage, but it was fortunately something we could overcome.

This surprise in our finances could have all been prevented had we run each other's credit report. If marriage is on the table, there should be full disclosure of each person's full financial situation accompanied by a credit report.

Though large amounts of debt may not be a deal breaker for your pending nuptials, you should at least know, upfront, what you're getting into. If possible, these money conversations should be pretty regular before and after marriage. In fact, I would say they should turn into planning sessions about how you're going to build a financial future together.

During this time, it's probably that the "spender" and "saver" roles will be identified. As you get to know one another, you'll start to see who can do what in the process of building your financial legacy. As you are able to define your roles, the plan to build wealth as a team will get clearer.

The saver gets security from having money piled up in the bank. As a joint-money protocol is developed for a marriage, there should be a savings plan to help the saver feel secure. This might include adding a line item in the budget for saving or automatically transferring money into a savings account each week. It also might mean setting up a number of savings accounts that correspond to irregular budget categories like car maintenance, vacation, gifts, property taxes, and so on. As the saver gets their needs met, they can feel more secure about meeting the needs of their spender partner.

For the spender, they should also be able to budget in their wants. The only thing about a spender is that they want to spend on lots of random things at times. So it's during these money meetings that you'll have to encourage the spender to choose one or two goals or even an amount of money a month that they can have to spend freely. Once those goals or dollar amounts are set, there should be a line item in the budget allocating money towards the spender's desires.

For us, this worked out by having different savings accounts. At one point, my husband told me that he wanted a classic car. I went ahead and opened an account and begin to contribute money on his behalf to the account. The balance got pretty high and after a few years he decided to use this money to replace his regular everyday car.

Using this money, we were able to get a car without having a car note. However, we still have this account open and I still contribute money to it so that he can have his dream of getting a classic car one day.

What it all boils down to is that the spender and the saver both have desires. When you have your money meetings, make sure that you incorporate the practical with the fun. And though everyone may not get exactly what they want, this is where the art of compromise comes in. It can make a marriage beautifully functional with the potential to accomplish many awesome things thanks to teamwork.

Make sure your money talk includes how you will manage money and what that will look like for your relationship. For example, you may decide to have a joint banking account and pay all the bills there. Or you may decide to have separate bank accounts and each person is responsible for a different set of bills.

You may also have a situation where you have monthly budget meetings to decide what to spend for which budget categories. Though you come together as a team to create the budget, maybe one person is responsible for executing. That is, he or she pays the bills and follows up with any issues that might arise in this household budget management process.

There are so many different arrangements that there is no one perfect or right way to do it. You'll just have to encourage your daughter to define the way that works for her and her potential mate and tweak it until it works for both of them.

We should also warn our daughters that the process of getting on the same page and mastering money as a couple could take time. It's a skill set that can take people many years to learn. It's like learning to salsa or tango. First, you have to learn the skill of dancing and then you have to know your partner. It may actually take a few rounds on the dance floor before you both become proficient at dealing with money as a team.

It's not uncommon to have fights or extreme tension when money is discussed. The important thing is not to take this as a sign of a weak or potentially failing marriage. It's actually a sign of a relationship that is developing and becoming more effective at problem-solving and making decisions for the greater good of the family.

Now when it comes to more practical matters regarding money and relationships, one of the most common concerns is about who should pay for what. If you are dating or in a courtship situation, going out to restaurants or movies can get pretty expensive. Young couples facing the burden of things like student loans, new bills, car notes, and rent could be overwhelmed by adding a "dating bill." Personally, I come from the "old school" and I think that the cost of dating should be primarily the man's responsibility. If money is an issue for him, perhaps dating should be held off until he is more financially stable. Another option is for him to find fun and inexpensive things to do. Creativity can go a long way if it comes from a sincere place of wanting to do better with one's finances while cultivating a relationship.

I'm a big believer that if someone cherishes who you are—your time, your energy, your personality—they will make time and find resources for you. No, it's not about the girl getting a free meal. It's more about gauging the true interest of a potential mate. The good book tells us, "For where your treasure is, there will your heart be also." Nothing could be closer to the truth!

When I began dating my husband, he paid for everything on our dates and even offered to pay for more. He'd put gas in my tank if I drove to see him. He would cover every meal and if I was out somewhere without a suitable outfit, he felt like it was his obligation to buy me one!

No one had ever done that for me, and to me, it was one of the ways he was expressing his love for me. These actions let me know that he cared deeply for me. When I compared his actions to the actions of other suitors, this along with many other things he did for me, solidified my confidence that he was *truly* into me.

I will say that I am a fan of using the willingness to spend time *and* money as one of many litmus tests to figure out if a man is truly interested. I'll leave that there, as opinions may differ on the matter, but it's a conversation that you should have with your daughter as she begins to date.

Next up, I think it's worth mentioning the idea of a prenuptial agreement. Now this is a tough one. Personally, I think there is no place for prenuptial agreements in a relationship because it sets a bad tone and a shaky foundation for marriage.

A prenuptial agreement basically says, "If it doesn't work out between us, this is how the finances will work in a divorce." I'm not a huge fan of the idea, because it begs the question: how much faith do you have in your relationship if you are setting an entire document in place to preserve your finances but not your relationship? It just seems like a move in bad faith that could spell disaster in a marriage.

But I do understand the other side of this issue and why a prenuptial agreement might be needed. For example, my daughters are already making money. It could very well be that by the time they get married, they could have built up a sizable net worth due to their acting activities (at least I hope that they do). How would I feel about them getting married to someone who might not have as much but could potentially take half or more of their earnings should the marriage not work out? Just the thought of that makes me uneasy.

Though I don't know that I would encourage them to have a prenuptial agreement, it's something that I think about. Hopefully, I'll raise my daughters to choose an exceptional mate who also brings an established net worth to the table. From there, I'd encourage them to seek the best for their marriage and their relationship. I would, however, totally understand if a prenuptial agreement was put in place.

On the flip side, there may be people who have *extremely* high net worth and they are more than a little paranoid about losing their money to a spouse that becomes an ex. Additionally, there are people who want this agreement in place to make sure their potential spouse is really in the relationship for love and not for personal gain. Again, I think it's just a conversation to have so you can discuss the pros and cons. Even if you can't recommend prenups either way, have the talk so that your daughter knows what she wants early on and why she wants it.

I also want to bring up an important issue that is receiving more awareness when it comes to relational finances. The topic of financial abuse is important because women are, most often, the victims of spousal abuse and unfortunately, victims of financial abuse as well. Financial abuse occurs when one partner controls money, withholds money, or attempts to use money as a tool to control their partner.

Other forms of financial abuse could include:

- Getting a partner fired
- Ruining a partner's credit
- Depleting savings or investments without permission
- Hiding money
- Blocking access to joint financial records and information
- Creating an abusive environment that prevents financial education, planning, or foresight

According to the Center for Financial Security, 99 percent of domestic violence cases also involved financial abuse. Fortunately, many organizations such as non-profits, employers, and private corporations are starting to recognize this issue by providing support and financial literacy to abuse survivors.

If you believe that you are experiencing financial abuse, contact the National Domestic Violence Hotline at 800-799-SAFE (7233).

Lastly, it's important to consider the impact that kids can have on money and a relationship. There was a study done by the Brookings Institute and coauthored by Ron Haskins and Isabel Sawhill, authors of the book *Creating an Opportunity Society*. They crunched US Census data and found that if people do these three things, they have only a 2 percent chance of falling into poverty:[4]

- Graduate from high school

---

4 Times-Union, The. "Three Rules for Staying out of Poverty." The Florida Times-Union, January 27, 2012. https://www.jacksonville.com/article /20120127/OPINION/801258741.

- Wait to get married until after 21 and do not have children until after being married
- Have a full-time job

Imagine that, having children under less than ideal circumstances can be a factor that contributes to poverty! Procreating is a decision that should not be taken lightly. In fact, I believe that it should be as carefully planned as possible. If I could do it all over again, I would have timed my childbearing years in a way that would have made more sense financially. Thankfully, all is well and things have worked in our favor, but I would pass on a different set of instructions to my daughters.

Kids can drastically change the money dynamic of marriage due to the impact they have on relationships and finances. Though the way people care for their children will vary, the constant should be a solid financial plan to support the kids.

Whether your daughter is single or she's in a romantic relationship, kids could be part of her life at some time or another. If she can start putting money away as a single person or as someone involved in a relationship, she'll be much better off in terms of being able to raise her family on her own terms.

I am fortunate enough that I was able to stay home and raise my kids even through homeschooling them for most of their academic career. Ideally, it would have been nice to have money in the bank to help this happen, but a series of other fortunate circumstances made it possible. For example, we inherited a home with no mortgage and I married someone who felt okay with me staying home and raising the kids while he was out working.

I am very glad that we're able to put away money for our kids early on if they want to make the same decision. Hopefully, they will not only have a house without a mortgage, but they will also have money in the bank by the time they are ready to settle down. Whether or not they decide to stay home with their kids will be their business, but either way, my goal is for them to have the money in place so they can do what their heart desires.

CHAPTER 18

Let's Talk Buying a Home

Let's talk about another one of my favorite subjects: buying a home. Homeownership and the American dream is something that has been drilled into our minds from a very young age. In fact, it's the entire reason why you go to college and get into a lucrative profession. You need a good job so you can have the income to save up a down payment and make regular monthly payments on your piece of the American dream.

If you remember the 2008 housing crisis, you will know that the American dream turned into the American nightmare pretty quickly for millions of people. Overnight, many people lost 50 percent or 60 percent of their stock portfolios while real estate values plummeted. Banks began being extremely tight-fisted with their lending, causing the economy to essentially seize up. It was the economic Armageddon we all knew would come sooner or later.

The problem with the 2008 recession was that it left a bad taste in many people's mouths in terms of home ownership and real estate investments in general. It was at this point that people determined real estate a risky investment, decreasing overall demand and values of homes across the nation.

To some extent I would have to agree with some of the folks who were "scared straight" by the whole ordeal. Many people were using their homes as retirement plans based off of an antiquated real estate market paradigm that showed trends of real estate appreciation. Even since 2008, many property values still have not recovered and many others remain underwater.

If you purchased a home a few years before the real estate bust, maybe you felt good about your decision. When 2008 hit, that $300,000 mortgage was financing a home only worth $200,000. Imagine being underwater on a loan to the tune of $100,000! I'd say that sounds like a bad investment, but it's the reality that many people are facing. I'll be honest, it also made me avoid investing in real estate as well.

Then I began to understand the role that real estate could and should play in someone's overall wealth-building strategy. I do believe in homeownership as a foundation for building wealth. However, that will all depend on the *way* you go about homeownership.

For example, if you purchase a home hoping that it will have appreciated after 20 years, that's not an absurd supposition. You may want to refinance the home and use the extra cash to pay off low high-interest debt, go on vacation, or even cover college tuition for your kids. It's a reasonable thing that people have done for years and years and years.

However, the risk factor is that we don't know that the appraised value of the home will be sustained in every market environment. In other words, it's hard to predict, 20 years out, what the value of your home will be and if you'll be able to refinance it in a way that furthers some of your financial goals. This is somewhat speculative and can be risky if your financial strategy is dependent upon your property appreciation.

To me, putting very little down on a home and then financing it over 20 or 30 years presents risks many people don't think about. There's just no way to tell what will happen with real estate this far out. Historically, we do tend to see property values appreciate and rents go up over time.

I think that you should encourage your daughters to invest in home ownership, but in a way where they take into account certain risks and wild cards that people can't always forecast. In this vein, they should definitely have a backup plan in the case that some of their assumptions don't pan out.

One of my favorite strategies to building wealth with real estate is with a house hacking strategy. House hacking is when you purchase a home and have tenants to help cover the mortgage. In some cases, you may even clear a profit.

In our case, we started house hacking by living with family members. At one point in our marriage, our mother came to live with us. She helped pay our rent and then we went to live with her once she purchased her own home. She was gracious enough to defer our rent so we could aggressively pay down debt. But can you see how this could work when family members get together and share household expenses? This shared-housing strategy leaves more money for each one to build wealth.

Once we moved into our own home, we began to host local college students in our downstairs rooms. We occupied the upstairs level while renters occupied the lower level. This extra money helped us reach financial goals like paying down debt or just having extra money around to save.

Eventually, we moved out of that house and rented out all of the rooms that now cover the mortgage for our new investment property. You can see that having renters and tenants is a way to use other people's money to build equity and property.

Currently, we are looking for another building. This time around, we'll get a multi-unit. We'll live in one unit and rent out the other couple of units so that our mortgage is covered. You can continue this, ad infinitum, until you amass a real estate empire.

This empire-building may not be your daughter's cup of tea. She might decide that regular old, run-of-the-mill homeownership will work better for her.

How Much to Put Down on a House

I think it makes sense to put 20 percent down on a home purchase in *some* cases. If you've got that money in savings and plan to pay down your home quickly, 20 percent down can help you avoid paying private mortgage insurance (PMI), which can be an extra $1,000 or more per year.

Another approach is to put down as *little* of your own money as possible. This can be done with loan products like the FHA loan. It allows you to put 3.5 percent down on your house purchase. The FHA 203k version allows you to get both a construction loan to rehab a property and purchase the home while putting only 3.5 percent down.

This makes sense when you don't have a lot of money saved up and will buy into some equity (meaning your home appraises for more than you buy it for). An example would be buying a home for $100,000 and putting $3,500 down (though adding closing costs might make it a couple thousand higher). If the home appraises at $150,000, you've just bought into $50,000 worth of home equity or ownership.

I like this method even more if you are able to get a multi-unit home. With an FHA loan, you are able to get up to four units with 3.5 percent down. To me, this is an incredibly smart way to be a home-owner should you decide to become one. Imagine just paying a few thousand dollars for a home, having renters to cover your mortgage, and having equity in your property by using very little of your own money.

Now, this approach sounds really smart, but it's not risk-free. For example, you may get a home that initially appraises well over the purchase price. However, if there is a drop in the market value, maybe due to lower demand, you will lose out on that equity you previously thought you bought into.

Another risk with the multi-unit route is that you may not find tenants or you have bad tenants. They could tear up your property or not pay their rent consistently. One way to mitigate this risk is by having a sufficient amount of savings in case of real estate emergencies.

Finally, this approach works provided you are responsible with your resources and have a long-term plan to turn your home into an investment. I am a big fan of home ownership, but I think there is a better way to do it if you're able to.

If you decide just to be a regular homeowner, it's totally acceptable to put down 20 percent or more and have a plan to pay off your mortgage sooner than later. You can do this by getting a 15- or 20-year mortgage.

You should also make sure that your mortgage is no more than 20 to 25 percent of your take-home pay. Then, you'll want to make sure that you keep an emergency fund to cover maintenance and repairs. If all this works for your budget, I think being a homeowner could be a good investment.

The key here is to make sure that there is an exit strategy or some other strategy to use that home to earn money in some way in the future. I think the home, in and of itself, is not the end goal, but it's what the home can provide—such as low-cost living, shelter, and further down the line, some equity and cash to accomplish other things—that makes it so valuable.

On the other hand, straightforward home ownership (that is, owning a home without having renters and just using it as a primary residence) still requires you to consider the total cost of owning that home. The mortgage note isn't the only expense included in home-ownership. There are maintenance costs associated with owning a home. There are also property, taxes, insurance, and then there's property upkeep.

To get a bill for $10,000 to fix your roof could be devastating. A homeowner doesn't want to walk away from his or her home because he or she can't afford the upkeep. If your daughter is purchasing a home, make sure that she understands that her mortgage should be a reasonable amount of her take-home pay. She should then add an extra couple hundred or more per month in her budget to save up for incidentals.

Home Ownership Isn't for Everyone

Yes, I'm a fan of using real estate to build wealth, but I realize that this kind of investment isn't for everyone. Maybe someone moves around a lot or doesn't really have much trust in the real estate market. That doesn't mean that he or she is ineligible to build wealth.

Your daughter's path to wealth building may just look a little different, and she shouldn't feel bad about it. The *New York Times* created a rent vs. buy calculator to help figure out if renting makes more sense. The calculator assumes that the money one saves from having a home is invested instead.

The calculator proves that in some cases, renters could actually fare better in retirement provided they take the money they would have saved on a home purchase and place it in investments that could grow into a sizeable nest egg.

So for example, let's say that the cost of homeownership ends up being $1,500 a month but your daughter is able to rent for $900 a month. With renting, she'd never have to pay any maintenance fees, property taxes, or any of the other surprises that can come with being a homeowner. If she were to take $600 or the difference between $1,500 and $900 and invest that in the stock market over 30 years or so, assuming a 5 percent rate of return, she could add an extra $478,359.70 to her retirement savings.

All in all, home ownership serves as a way to force people to save their money and have an asset that they also can get some use out of. If your daughter doesn't think that homeownership is for her, help her talk through a plan to use the money she saves as a renter on investments like the stock market, business holdings, or some other way to make the money grow over time.

CHAPTER 19

Let's Talk Giving Back

One great thing about the time we live in is that this generation is obsessed in the best way with giving back and living a life of purpose. It's not enough just to vacation. This generation likes to volunteer *while* vacationing. Companies are offering days off to employees that volunteer their time and participate in service projects. Companies like TOMS and Warby Parker have built giving back into their business model.

As I pointed out in the beginning of the book, we know that when women earn more money they have a more sizable impact on charitable causes. They tend to give more, volunteer more, and use their compassion and empathy to help those in need.

When we talk to our daughters about their money situation and where they see themselves years from now, we must include giving in the conversation. It's crucial for the advancement of a compassionate, empathetic world designed to help the needy among us. That's the real reason for wealth—to help the world become a better place.

Aunties, mothers, grandmothers, cousins, or women—anyone who can influence a younger woman—must frame the money conversation so its purpose is clear: money is a tool to bless, uplift, and help others. Even if you think you failed in terms of using your resources and income to help others, now is a good time to have that conversation with your daughter so that you can start the tradition of giving back as a lifestyle in your family.

Having this conversation with your daughter doesn't mean that you've mastered the art of giving back; it just means that you're thinking about it more and you want to involve her on your journey.

Before we talk about some important topics in regards to giving, I'll tell you a little bit about how our family structures giving. I'll also tell you a little about how we encourage our daughters to give out of their earnings as well as giving back as a family.

We are Christian and therefore we subscribe to the biblical principle of tithing. That means we give 10 percent of our earnings to our church. Our church, in turn, supports missionaries, orphanages, water well projects, entrepreneurial training centers in other countries, as well as other churches in various countries that also support the same things. We feel good about giving to our church because we can see, firsthand, some of the ways they invest in people around the world.

Even if you aren't a Christian and don't believe in the idea of tithing, it's not a bad idea to set aside a percentage of your earnings or even your time for charitable causes. My frame of reference is from the Bible. There is this principle of giving explained in Luke 6:38: "Give, and it will be given to you. A good measure, pressed down, shaken together and running over, will be poured into your lap. For with the measure you use, it will be measured to you" (NIV).

From this verse, I teach my daughters that as they give and help and bless others, then they will also be blessed. There is another scriptural principle that echoes the same sentiment, Proverbs 11:25: "The liberal soul shall be made fat: and he that watereth shall be watered also himself" (KJV).

In other words, think about a water hose that transports water from the spigot to an end destination like the front lawn. As water runs through that hose, it's bound to get wet.

This principle applies to the giver. The woman who makes up her mind to be an intentional giver will also receive gifts and blessings.

As my daughters earn their money, we immediately take out money that goes towards giving. Before any bills are paid or any other financial priorities are addressed, the 10 percent comes out to be a blessing to others.

Fortunately, my daughters have never lacked the funds to pay their bills. Granted, they are only 10 and 14 years old, so they don't have many bills. But due to their careers in acting they do have to pay for union fees, headshots, coaching, and other things related to their craft.

People are amazed at the amount of money they've been able to amass in such a short period of time with the small and medium-sized gigs that they've booked. Yet whenever it looked like they were going through a dry spell, we would set our minds on giving in order to break it. And would you believe, like clockwork, every time they made up their minds to take a portion of their earnings to be a blessing to someone else, the work would start up again!

You might be thinking, sure that works for some little kids that really don't have many expenses and don't live paycheck-to-paycheck. While that is partly true, I have plenty of other examples where my husband and I implemented giving in order to break dry spells in our business efforts, too. In fact, the reason why we have two businesses, own real estate, and have had a blessed, prosperous life is mainly due to our commitment to giving.

Building Giving Back into Your Lifestyle

As mentioned, there are many ways to build giving back into your lifestyle. The ways we can encourage our daughters to give is by modeling a lifestyle of giving. We should also be sure to communicate about the flexible forms that giving can take on.

There have been times when I didn't have much money to give, even though I had the heart to give. It was in these moments that I ended up giving my time and the results were still just as powerful. Not only was I able to be a blessing to others by being present and being helpful, but also I reaped the benefits of prospering as a result of blessing someone else.

Building giving back into your lifestyle can be setting aside a portion of your income. Our giving target is 10 percent. If you can't give 10 percent, think about starting at 1 percent. From there, you can increase it as you feel comfortable. Once you start, you'll start to see that giving sets off a domino effect of prosperity and blessing in your life and in the lives of others. I guarantee you, at some point, you will probably be encouraged to keep going and increase your giving levels.

Another way to build giving back into our lifestyles includes dedicating a portion of our time. This could be a regular volunteer commitment or something less frequent. If it's difficult to find places to volunteer, there are plenty of websites that can connect you to organizations and causes that align with your passion.

Giving back doesn't always have to take that form, though. We can have elderly relatives in our lives or our neighborhoods that would love to have our companionship and assistance. Maybe you've got a relative who just had a baby or just experienced something very difficult in their lives and could just use a listening ear or a helping hand. They should be candidates to receive your help as well.

During that giving talk, help your daughters consider the people close by just as much as they'd think about a more formal volunteering opportunity.

Even when you are in a difficult place, giving back and helping others tends to improve your quality of life overall, which can definitely impact your finances in a positive way.

If you haven't yet set up a good system for giving back, there's no time like the present. Talk with your daughters and be accountable with one another about your commitment to give back and be a blessing to others. You can even start family traditions to establish a family culture of giving. The goal isn't to necessarily give a whole lot but rather to start where you are and give what you can and out of what you have.

CHAPTER 20

Let's Talk Having Fun

There's plenty of talk about living your best life. In fact, if you go to Instagram, you'll see that the platform is chock-full of influencers, movie stars, and other high-profile people who happily display the highlight reels of their lives. They travel, do awesome things with their kids, and are making a difference in the world.

This generation is no stranger to living a decadent, pleasure-filled life. Even though it seems like our culture is inundated with these images of the high life, it's not all bad.

The wisest man in the world, King Solomon of the Bible, even saw the importance of a man being able to enjoy the fruits of his labor: "There is nothing better for a man, than that he should eat and drink, and that he should make his soul enjoy good in his labour. This also I saw, that it was from the hand of God" (Ecclesiastes 2:24).

Having the opportunity and the capability to earn money, make a difference, and create a good life for ourselves is one of the greatest gifts and blessings from God. Therefore, we should encourage our daughters to make sure they incorporate rest, relaxation, and fun into the life they will build with the fruits of their labor.

It's not uncommon for women to feel guilty for having fun. We've been groomed, for many centuries, to be the caretakers of all those around us. So when it comes to setting aside time for ourselves and for self-care, it can be difficult to actually do it without a guilty conscious—especially for our daughters who will go on to become mothers, aunties, and matriarchs of the family. We are conditioned to sacrifice ourselves and feel guilty when fun comes into the equation. But a life without fun will eventually lead to burnout, stress, and even illness.

Just like you would budget time and money to go to the doctor or the grocery store, you'll want to encourage your daughter to budget time for fun as well. In fact, depending on her lifestyle and her personality type, she may even want to consider building fun into many aspects of her life, including her job, raising her kids, and taking care of business in general.

Personally, I know that it is difficult for me to have a very structured schedule. It is precisely for this reason that I chose to become a writer and marketer so that I could work from home.

There are times when I'm legitimately tired and I don't have the bandwidth to do a lot of work. Sometimes, I have taken off as many as two, three, or four weeks at a time. And it's not always for fun. Sometimes it's just for rest and recharging.

Fun doesn't sound like a financial concept, but it really is. As mentioned before in the chapter about entrepreneurial burnout, this actually applies to our daughters that may not ever become entrepreneurs. They'll live their lives as women in this world and could still be subject to constant burnout due to the demands placed on them by their families, their jobs, and society as a whole.

Fun and responsibility don't have to be mutually exclusive either. In fact, I would argue that building fun into one's life, schedule, and budget is one of the most financially responsible things that one can do for oneself. After all, what good is money if people run themselves into the ground and never get to enjoy their hard-earned cash?

When you are talking with your daughter, discuss the importance of balance when it comes to work and play. Help her talk through what it might look like to have a good work to rest ratio along with the practical application as it relates to her schedule and financial resources.

CHAPTER 21

How to Maintain Self-Love through Good Money Management

As I mentioned earlier in the book, how we deal with money can be a reflection of how we are doing in terms of self-love, self-worth, self-esteem, etc. I'll say it again: money is neither good nor bad. It can be a reflection of who you already are and how you feel about yourself.

Many times, when we are bad with money, it's a reflection of how we feel about ourselves. Maybe we don't feel worthy enough to put aside funds for things like self-care, retirement, or health and wellness.

Maybe we spend a lot of money trying to make ourselves look better. There's so much money that can be spent on outward appearance that we sometimes neglect our inward being in the process. Yes, we can spend all the money in the world on looking pretty, but if we're not pretty on the inside, what have we accomplished?

With our daughters, it seems like we are constantly discussing self-esteem and self-love. Living in the age of social media and doctored-up images can make it even tougher for us to teach our daughters to be proud of who they are, just the way they are.

If we are looking to money to provide our self-worth, it's just not possible. We've got to know that we are worthy of an abundant, prosperous life no matter what. There will be times when we do well with money and there will be times when we do badly with money. This doesn't mean that we are a bad person. It doesn't mean that we are not worthy to work toward improving ourselves and our financial situation.

Using money as a form of self-love is not the same as self-worship. When you use money to love yourself, it becomes a tool that will help you accomplish your God-given purpose. It's nothing more and nothing less.

I think we need to give ourselves permission to see money in that way. We don't have to put it on a pedestal so that we obsess over it incessantly, but we don't have to ignore it with the belief that material things just don't matter. That's not true. Money is a resource and a tool and it's needed for us to accomplish things. If we use the proper protocols and give money the proper place in our lives, it can be a wonderful resource for ourselves and our daughters to make the world a better place.

Building Self-Esteem through Positive Activities

One way to love ourselves through our financial resources is to engage in activities that build our self-esteem. Of course, activities should not be the final measure of our self-worth, but there are some activities that are definitely worthy of our time and others that are not.

(We are talking about money, but in many cases time does equal money. The time that we spend doing things can be money that we either earn or forgo, so I'm okay with including the way we spend our time in this discussion.)

Activities that build your self-esteem can include gainful employment, volunteering, being creative, and being constructive. There are some activities that are not worth our time because they use resources and creativity that could be better applied elsewhere.

For example, gossiping and talking about other people is a poor use of time and also shows that we don't love ourselves and have low self-esteem. It means we have to put down others so that we can feel better about ourselves.

Another poor use of our time is catering to people who will ultimately drain our energy or keep us from growing in the way we should. Unfortunately, many times our close friends and family members are the biggest offenders. As women, we have the special ability to sacrifice ourselves and nurture others. However, Many times we will help others when we ourselves are drowning.

I do believe there is a time and place for constructive self-sacrifice. But there is this idea of putting on your own oxygen mask so that you can help others around you. I had to learn that the hard way. There are some activities you won't be able to participate in because you've got a higher calling on your life. After all, if your ship sinks, how many people will you be able to help?

If you are in a situation where you have friends and family members that constantly interrupt your day asking for your time to do things that are not necessarily constructive or in line with your purpose, it's okay to respect yourself and love yourself and say no. You may not be able to get everyone from the airport. You may not be able to pet-sit your neighbor's dog for their next vacation.

Yes, you can still be a nice person and say no because you have boundaries. These boundaries will preserve your energy and help you walk in your calling without fatigue, irritability, and constant pressures to quit and give up.

Loving yourself and respecting yourself will mean protecting the resources you have like time, energy, and even your money. Everyone is not worthy of the precious resources that you've spent years honing and cultivating.

You're not selfish. You are practicing self-care and self-preservation. I think the tradeoff is fair and worth it.

Financial Independence, Alone or with a Mate

Another way to use money as a way to express self-love is to understand that successful money management can happen on your own and it can also happen should you decide to marry. You can be a successful independent woman or a successful interdependent woman with a spouse, and both can be equally satisfying and great accomplishments.

I remember as a teenager and in my early twenties, one of my biggest goals was to marry a man of means. I imagined myself with some ballplayer or politician or even the pastor of a megachurch. Looking back, I realize that you can absolutely build wealth with someone along the way. While there's nothing necessarily wrong with having aspirations to "marry up," we should not rule out potential mates who don't necessarily meet those lofty financial ideas but rather have the potential to get there with time.

Personally, I feel blessed to have experienced the process of my husband and I building wealth together. I know that there are many stories of successful couples where the man (or woman) is already wealthy and they are happy to bring in their spouse to the fold, but in some situations this type of union can be a point of contention between spouses. One spouse may feel like they don't bring enough to the table while the other one may not trust the motivations of the spouse who "married up."

I'm not saying that you shouldn't marry someone who has more money than you. However, it's a decision that should not be taken lightly. I tell my daughters, "If you happen to meet someone that happens to be a man of means, then feel free to pursue a relationship and if it continues into marriage that's totally fine." But to base your marriage desires on financial status could end up being disastrous.

I tell my daughters that they are more than capable of making all the money they will need for their "wealthy place." As I heard one woman put it, "I became the doctor that my mother always wanted me to marry." You can fill in the blank and become whatever it is you aspired to marry into. From here, you'll attract the type of mate that sees someone who already has their own self-worth, self-value, self-love, and self-respect.

Another way to love yourself through money is to hang among social circles that affirm your financial goals. As you become very clear on the vision for your life and the goals that you have for yourself, your circle of friends should reflect that. It will be hard to get to that wealthy place with people who don't want that for themselves.

For instance, if you are looking to build a real estate empire, it's going to take time, energy, and money. If you hang with people who always find a reason to spend money recreationally—whether it's through excessive travel, going to bars and nightclubs, or constantly taking shopping trips, it will be hard to stick to your goal of real estate investing. You'll always be tempted to spend your time and money in other places that don't align with your financial goals.

For this reason, you'll probably see your inner circle changing. If you don't consciously change your inner circle, then your financial goals could suffer. Hang with people who have similar goals, and they'll understand the healthy boundaries that you have to put in your life. Our daughters may even witness us change our inner circle of friends as we go through different stages of our lives.

Having Financial Integrity

Another way to love yourself through wise financial decisions is by having financial integrity. Just as I was writing this last chapter, I thought it would be nice to book a trip for my husband and me to go to Aruba. I wanted to celebrate our 15th anniversary and the completion of this manuscript.

And though I was able to find pretty inexpensive tickets and accommodations, I quickly remembered that I had some outstanding medical and therapy bills to pay. Before I made this move, I went to my online portals to make those payments.

These bills are not urgent, and I probably could have waited a few more months to make sure they got paid, but as a business owner and as a Christian, I like the idea of paying people when I'm able to. After all, I want to sow seeds of prompt, on-time payment and good business practices because I want others to do the same to me.

When I think about having financial integrity, a couple of Bible scriptures come to mind:

Proverbs 3:27–28:

"27 Do not withhold good from those to whom it is due, when it is in your power to act.

28 Do not say to your neighbor, 'Come back tomorrow and I'll give it to you'—when you already have it with you." (KJV).

Matthew 7:12 tells us, "So in everything, do to others what you would have them do to you, for this sums up the Law and the Prophets" (KJV).

We expect people to treat us justly and fairly. We have this expectation because we hold ourselves in high regard and (ideally) have a high sense of self-worth. However, in return, we need to treat others with the same respect.

Financial integrity is something that has to be developed and it does take practice. Even as a seasoned personal finance speaker, author, and blogger, I sometimes struggle with financial integrity myself.

I admit that there have been some bills that I've let slip through my fingers and probably taken longer than I should have to pay. I'll be out enjoying myself, even with the knowledge that I have outstanding financial obligations. It doesn't happen as often as it used to, but it's something that I still try to stay on top of because ultimately I want to be the recipient of fair financial practices.

Pay Yourself

Financial integrity can take on many forms. It's not just paying bills on time. Financial integrity also means paying yourself. Truth be told, we spend lots of money helping build the empires and fortunes of many other people and companies. But financial integrity says that we must also invest money into ourselves.

If you love yourself and value yourself, you know that it's important to have a financial cushion. This is an emergency fund or some type of savings so that you don't stress yourself out. Stress remediation is definitely a form of self-care and self-love.

Financial integrity also means loving your *future* self. This means having a plan so that your future self is well taken care of. When you love your future self, you're also loving the people around you. Create an estate plan, obtain proper insurance coverage, make a will. Do whatever it takes to get your financial ducks in a row so you can be taken care of in the moments you'll need it most. The last thing you want is to become a burden on your friends and family because you didn't have enough financial integrity to put away money when you could.

Be Patient with Yourself

Finally, a great way to love yourself with money is to give yourself grace. When we talk to our daughters about money, we want to let them know that learning to handle money in a way that serves their purpose is complicated and emotional. It can take time to master.

When we talk about managing money, we must also talk about giving ourselves grace. We must communicate to our daughters that no money damage is irreparable and that anyone can bounce back from even the biggest money mistake.

There might even be times when we mess up terribly with money. We may even give our daughters bad money advice or model bad financial behavior. However, it's never too late to recognize our mistakes and start all over again.

I know I've said this plenty of times throughout the book, but one of the best conversations we can have with our daughters is how we made our own money mistakes and how we bounced back from those mistakes. Our daughters are people before they are anything else. Thus, our daughters are not always looking for perfection but rather advice regarding how we deal with our imperfections. This can be applied to money management as well!

This talk about grace with our daughters means giving them the room to make mistakes and the hope and inspiration it takes to recover and start anew.

Finally, we must also remember that these money conversations are not the final destination. As moms, we tend to fuss with our young people hoping they will be compelled to act on all the advice we give them. In the end, we can't make anyone do anything. We all know the old adage, "You can lead a horse to water, but you can't make him drink."

As we discuss money with our daughters, we're just leading them to water. We're starting conversations and planting the seeds of hope, change, and money management positivity into their minds. Seeds take time to grow. So give *yourself* grace if your money messages don't always seem to resonate with your daughters.

I know that I've spent hours upon hours talking to my kids, probably incessantly, about different financial concepts. Sometimes they'll get their allowances and within hours it's already been spent! When this happens, it's easy for me to get discouraged and wonder if anything I'm doing is even making a difference with my daughters.

This reminds me of the time I was teaching my three-year-old how to write the letter *A*. We spent the better part of an hour yelling and going back and forth about the fact that she had the hand-eye coordination to write the letter *A* on her own.

I fussed and we fought. It was at this point that I had seriously considered leaving parenting alone. If this was any indication on how I was going to handle parenthood, obviously I was doomed and so was my daughter.

After a while we could fight and fuss no longer. There was not a single *A* written on the page that we had labored over for the last hour. I was exhausted. I was discouraged and disgusted. How could I fail teaching my daughter one of the most simple letters of the alphabet?

It's a letter made up of three lines, for crying out loud! I also knew that my oldest daughter had relatively good fine motor skills for her age, so I was surprised that she was being so stubborn and didn't want to cooperate.

It was a hard afternoon for me. We eventually decided to call it quits and we went our separate ways. I went upstairs, maybe to do some cleaning or playing around on the computer, and my daughter went to another part of the house to play with her aunt.

After a couple of hours, I emerged to look for my daughter to see what she had been up to. I looked in the driveway to find about 100 capital letter *A*s in different color chalk on the asphalt!

I looked for my daughter, and she was nowhere to be found. Then, I went around the house and eventually found her in her aunt's room. (We were all living with my mom at the time.) Here, she was carefully making letter *A*s with small wooden sticks. You know, the rattan ones that people use with essential oils.

She got it!

Truthfully, I was extremely relieved to see all those letter *A*s. Even though we had fought for a long time, she was still soaking up the information I was giving her, but for whatever reason wasn't ready to act on it in that moment. I had a good laugh that day and I still remember that story every time I hunker down to fuss with my daughters about some type of money lesson I think they should be learning.

The point is that when you are planting seeds, they may not look like "full trees" of financial knowledge right away. As I've said throughout this book, our job is simply to plant those seeds. We can water them with more conversations, but we'll have to trust the process. We must trust that those seeds will grow into the living, breathing organisms they were designed to be.

That mother-daughter or auntie-niece or older-younger cousin dynamic can get a little sticky. Our pride can get in the way and it's hard to be vulnerable and open to correction on both sides of those mentor-mentee relationships.

In the end, we'll have to be patient and gentle with each other as we navigate money topics among our female cohorts. When we start these conversations, it should be our goal to see them be better with money and finances than we ever were. Of course, that is what we want them to pass on to their daughters as well.

Index

Books from Allworth Press

Estate Planning (in Plain English)*
by Leonard D. DuBoff and Amanda Bryan (6 × 9, 240 pages, paperback, $19.99)

Feng Shui and Money (Second Edition)
by Eric Shaffert (6 × 9, 256 pages, paperback, $19.99)

How to Avoid Probate for Everyone
by Ronald Farrington Sharp (5½ × 8¼, 192 pages, paperback $14.99)

Legal Forms for Everyone (Sixth Edition)
by Carl Battle (8½ × 11, 280 pages, paperback, $24.99)

Living Trusts for Everyone (Second Edition)
by Ronald Farrington Sharp (5½ × 8¼, 192 pages, paperback $14.99)

Love & Money
by Ann-Margaret Carrozza with foreword by Dr. Phil McGraw (6 × 9, 240 pages, paperback, $19.99)

The Money Mentor
by Tad Crawford (6 × 9, 272 pages, paperback, $24.95)

Protecting Your Assets from Probate and Long-Term Care
by Evan H. Farr (6 × 9, 208 pages, paperback, $14.99)

Quadrant Life
by Lori Dennis (5½ × 8¼, 216 pages, hardcover, $14.99)

Scammed
by Gini Graham Scott, PhD (6 × 9, 256 pages, paperback, $16.99)

The Secret Life of Money
by Tad Crawford (5½ × 8½, 304 pages, paperback, $19.95)

The Smart Consumer's Guide to Good Credit
by John Ulzheimer (5¼ × 8¼, 216 pages, paperback, $14.95)

To see our complete catalog or to order online, please visit *www.allworth.com*.